INVITATION TO

MEDITERRANEAN COOKING

CLAUDIA RODEN was born and brought up in Cairo. She finished her education in Paris and later studied art in London. Starting as a painter she was drawn to the subject of food partly through a desire to evoke a lost heritage – one of the pleasures of a happy life in Egypt. With her bestselling classic, *A Book of Middle Eastern Food*, first published in 1968, Claudia Roden revolutionized Western attitudes to the cuisines of the Middle East. Her most recent publication is the highly acclaimed *The Book of Jewish Food*.

Also in the Pan Cooks series

Claudia Roden

Invitation to Mediterranean Cooking

PAN BOOKS

First published 1997 by Pavilion Books

This edition published 2002 by Pan Books
an imprint of Pan Macmillan Ltd
20 New Wharf Road, London N1 9RR
Basingstoke and Oxford
Associated companies throughout the world
www.panmacmillan.com

ISBN 0 330 39169 0

9 8 7 6 5 4 3 2 1

A CIPcatalogue record for this book is available from
the British Library.

Typeset by SX Composing DTP, Rayleigh, Essex
Printed and bound in Great Britain by
Mackays of Chatham plc, Chatham, Kent

For my children, Simon, Nadia and Anna,

and for Ros and Clive who have joined the family

— with my thanks for eating through the book with me

Contents

Introduction

The Mediterranean Diet – A Model of Healthy Eating

In the late 1960s the world became aware of the work of the American nutritionist Ancel Keys, who studied the link between diet and disease of men in seven countries and found that almost all the countries around the Mediterranean had a lower rate of cardiovascular diseases, cancer and various other chronic diseases. His discoveries triggered a flood of research in all corners of the world. Some countries, such as Italy and Finland, changed the diet of whole villages and noted the results. Immigrant communities whose eating habits changed in new homelands were also studied.

Although there are many contradictions and confusion in nutritional theories, the results of these studies showed that despite other factors, such as genetics, lifestyle and environment, diet remained the obvious major cause of disease. The so-called Western diseases of affluence were linked to a diet low in fibre, high in sugar and saturated animal fats; and the diet of the Mediterranean countries – rich in grains, vegetables, fruit and nuts, with plenty of fish and little meat, and oil as the main cooking fat – came out as the ideal healthy diet.

A worldwide consensus gradually emerged about what to eat. The World Health Organization, the Food and Agriculture Organization and all the major world-health reports have come up with the same recommendations: eat more wheat, rice, beans, lentils, chick peas and nuts, lots of fresh vegetables and fruit, more fish, less red meat, and cook with oil rather than butter. Many governments have issued food guidelines based on these recommendations.

Recently, olive oil has been heralded as an effective weapon in the fight against disease. Since time immemorial, it has been believed to have curative and nutritive properties – a panacea for all kinds of illnesses – and modern science has confirmed its beneficial qualities. It is high in monounsaturated fats and fatty acids and rich in vitamin E, which is an antioxidant that is believed to help prevent heart and lung diseases and cancer. Like all vegetable and seed oils, it is cholesterol free. And it has the added effect of reducing so-called 'bad' cholesterol (low-density lipoproteins) and increasing 'good' cholesterol (high-density lipoproteins).

Of course, other parts of the world where people use large quantities of oil, vegetables, fruits and pulses could have been used as a model for healthy eating, but the Mediterranean style has been adopted as the best way to encourage people to change their eating habits because of its very special appeal. Mediterranean food is full of flavour, aroma and colour; and it is familiar enough for us to feel comfortable with on an everyday basis. The area was, after all, the cradle of Western civilization and it has always been the foremost tourist destination. Furthermore, this corner of the world is so immensely seductive, with its blue sea and sky, magical light and scented air, fairs and street markets, open-air terraces, and casual and leisurely good-humoured way of life, that it represents an art of living and eating that we would like to emulate.

A Culinary Renaissance

For years, in restaurants and hotels around the Mediterranean, local cooking has been overshadowed by French classic cuisine. When tourism was born at the end of the nineteenth century and high society discovered the Côte d'Azur, the luxury hotels and restaurants adopted the grand style of French gastronomy; this became the model to which the hospitality trade across the entire Mediterranean, and indeed the world, aspired.

In more recent times, the move from countryside to towns, the mass-production of food, the arrival of convenience and fast foods, and mass tourism have all contributed to the loss of traditional regional cooking. A French sociologist remarked cynically that *la cuisine du terroir* (the regional cooking of the land) exists only in cookery books. But it is not quite so. Nostalgia for a vanishing heritage and the fear of losing cultural identity, as well as a general change of tastes and values, have resulted in a revival of interest in regional rustic cuisines and in cottage industries, not only in France but in all the countries around the Mediterranean.

The top French chefs in Provence and the Côte d'Azur who went through their Nouvelle Cuisine rebellion against 'mummified Parisian classicism', have now turned to regional produce and styles for inspiration for their creations. In Italy, where *piatti tipici*, as they call local regional dishes, began to appear on restaurant menus little more than a decade ago, professional cooks say they want to update and revitalize the old dishes, not embalm them. They call the trend *il recupero* and *la riscoperta*. In every country around the Mediterranean, including Turkey, Egypt, Morocco and Tunisia, restaurants that had once been ashamed to offer anything but French and international classics are now proud to serve their own local dishes.

Another phenomenon is the way Mediterranean foods, especially the rustic, country and 'poor' foods, have become fashionable all over the world and are considered representative of 'modern' cooking. Star chefs in Britain and America are inspired by the produce and styles of the Mediterranean, and supermarkets stock all the necessary ingredients. It is especially gratifying to see how healthy eating and the pleasures of the table have converged.

In the beginning interest was focused on the cooking of southern Italy and Provence. More recently it has spread to all the varied cuisines of the area, and in particular to the more exotic ones of the eastern and southern Mediterranean.

Mediterranean Cuisine – A Many-Splendoured Thing

Although Mediterranean dishes are extraordinarily varied and there are many cooking styles in the sixteen or so countries around the little inland sea, there is a certain unity throughout the Mediterranean basin, which means that if you know one cuisine you will be able to understand the others, and many of the dishes can be seen as variations on a theme. The unity has to do with the sharing of climate and produce, with the intense traffic and trading activity between all the port cities, and with an incestuous history.

Since ancient times, settlers, colonizers and empires have spread across the entire area, introducing new produce, utensils and methods, and leaving their mark everywhere. The first wave of colonists – the Phoenicians, Greeks and Romans – established the trinity of wheat, olives and vines. The Arabs, who were the dominant force from the seventh century (they occupied part of Spain for 700 years and Sicily for 200), established new trading systems and spread the cultivation of foods such as rice, sugar cane, apricots and oranges (bitter oranges and lemons were known to the Romans), pomegranates, dates, bananas, artichokes, spinach and aubergines. Other important influences were the kingdom of Catalunya, which conquered Sicily, Sardinia and Naples and penetrated the south of France; and the crown of Aragon, which had possessions around the Mediterranean. The Normans and the Republic of Venice, which had colonies as far away as Alexandria, also introduced their cooking styles to the Mediterranean shores. One of the greatest unifying forces was the Ottoman Empire, which lasted for 500 years until its collapse in the early twentieth century. It spread a style of cooking, drawn from its conquered territories, to all the countries in the empire.

Apart from empires and colonists, movements of populations contributed to an interchange of cooking styles: for instance, the Moors returning to North Africa after their expulsion from Spain; Tunisians moving to Palermo to build the cathedral; Sicilian peasants brought to Algeria by the French colonists to work the land. And travellers went to and fro: troubadours and jongleurs from southern France were seen in Italy and Catalonia; spice merchants and itinerant traders were seen everywhere. More recently, the French pieds noirs, resettling in the south of France, and immigrant workers from North Africa have had an enormous impact.

A unified culinary culture was woven from these intermeshed threads, which made the Mediterranean a world of its own and has meant that Andalusia, Provence and southern Italy have more in common with their maritime neighbours than with the northern regimes of their own countries. Throughout the Mediterranean, cooks use the same clay pots, the same wood-burning ovens, pestles and mortars, skewers and grills. You find similar dishes – vegetables cooked in olive oil and eaten cold, stuffed vegetables, thick vegetable omelettes, rice dishes, creamy puddings and almondy pastries, and the same tomato sauce, which is the signature of Mediterranean cuisine. The olive tree has a strong historical and cultural association with the Mediterranean, and the juice pressed from olives is the traditional cooking oil of the region; although not all the countries use it exclusively, it is certainly used liberally, as is lemon juice. Most recipes call for garlic, though not usually in very large amounts and always in a way that softens the flavour, and herbs and spices add a beguiling touch. Combine this with the visual appeal of ingredients like peppers, tomatoes, orange pumpkin and black olives, and you get something quite enchanting.

There are, of course, also many differences that distinguish one country's cuisine from another's. Where the French use cognac, Sicilians use Marsala and Spaniards use sherry. Where Italians use pecorino (Romano) cheese or ricotta, the French use goats' cheese or Gruyère, and the Greeks and Turks use feta. While a fish soup in the French Midi is flavoured with orange peel and saffron, in Italy it is flavoured with white wine, peperoncino (chilli) and parsley, and in Tunisia with cumin, paprika, cayenne and coriander leaves. Parsley, coriander and mint are favourite herbs in the eastern Mediterranean, while basil and marjoram are favourites in the western part. A western Mediterranean dish may use vanilla or grated orange zest in place of the eastern Mediterranean orange blossom or rosewater and cinnamon. Egyptians mix fried garlic with crushed coriander seeds, and Turks combine cinnamon with allspice.

From the wealth of dishes of the area, I have picked only personal favourites. My concern was not to cover all the countries or to feature famous dishes or include an example of every type of food. It was to offer fresh, light, delicious, casual food for every day that is quick and easy to cook, as well as some more elaborate, exuberant dishes that are ideal for entertaining and special occasions and are fun to serve. Although the dishes are naturally in line with the ideals of healthy eating, the *pleasures* of cooking and eating are the main focus of this book.

Although there are no meat dishes in the book, the aim is to appeal to meat-eaters who wish to vary and extend their diet as well as to vegetarians. Meat has never featured largely in Mediterranean cooking. It was very highly prized, but the peasantry could hardly ever afford it. In some countries it was eaten only once a week, and sometimes only on festive occasions. In Christian countries, the medieval Church forbade meat on Fridays and during Lent, so for almost a third of the year, fish and legumes took the place of meat. Fish was prepared in a simple way, but a great deal of inventiveness and ingenuity went into creating vegetable dishes. Luckily, the area was blessed with a propitious climate and soil, and provided a wide variety of vegetables, nuts and fruit. That is why the Mediterranean is an Eden for vegetarians.

Tips from a Mediterranean Kitchen

Planning a Vegetarian Meal

The book has been organized in short chapters to make it easy to select a vegetarian menu. Each chapter, except Vegetable Side Dishes, Desserts and Basics, contains recipes for good main dishes. A light summer meal can consist of a salad or two served with good bread, accompanied, if you like, with cheese, while a simple winter meal can be soup with bread. A family meal may be one dish such as a pasta, risotto or bulgur pilaf, an egg dish, cheese bake, tart, flan or gratin, served with a salad and followed by fresh fruit.

For a small dinner party, have a soup or appetizer to start with, and cheese and a dessert to follow. There are dishes, such as vegetable couscous, that can be served as a one-dish meal. For a grander affair for many people, you may like to serve a variety of appetizers and a main dish, which can be made in advance and reheated if necessary.

The Mediterranean way is to end a meal with fresh fruit, but I have included many desserts because we in the Anglo-Saxon world are particularly fond of them. At dinner parties, especially, people look forward to a sweet dessert. Most of the desserts in this book are made with fruits that celebrate the produce of the Mediterranean.

Planning a Fish or Seafood Meal

A fish soup accompanied by toasted bread can be a meal in itself, followed by fruit or a dessert. Or you can plan around a seafood pasta, couscous or fish flan. The most common Mediterranean way is to grill or fry fish as simply as possible. A marinade or dressing is the usual embellishment, while sauces are provided as accompaniments. You can start the meal with a vegetable soup or appetizer or with seafood such as prawns, scallops or mussels. Serve the fish with a salad or with one of the many vegetable, rice or bulgur side dishes featured in this book.

About the Ingredients

Bulgur (cracked wheat): Also called *pourguri* in Cyprus and *burghul* in the Arab world, bulgur is wheat that has been boiled and dried, then ground to various degrees of fineness.

Couscous: Hard wheat that has been ground to various degrees of fineness, then moistened and coated with fine flour. It is cooked by steaming. The varieties available in this country are mass-produced and pre-cooked.

Flat-leafed parsley: The parsley of the Mediterranean region is the flat-leafed variety, which has a different flavour from our curly-leafed parsley. But curly-leafed parsley may be substituted if flat-leafed parsley is unavailable.

Harissa: A fiery hot chilli and garlic paste with spices from North Africa which can be bought from supermarkets and Middle Eastern stores. It is best bought in a tube rather than in a tin as you need only a little at a time. To make it yourself, see page 268.

Olives: Olives are a symbol of the Mediterranean. They all ripen from green and yellow, through red and violet, to purple and black. Cured and preserved black and green olives are served as appetizers and for breakfast, to accompany bread and cheese, and also go into many dishes. It is important to choose a good-tasting variety. Try sampling a few different types; every Mediterranean country produces some very good ones. The fleshy Greek Kalamata, the Spanish Manzanilla, the small black

Taggiasca from Liguria, and large green Cerignola of Puglia in Italy are famous, as are the sweet black wrinkled olives of Provence and the tiny ones of Nice. Unfortunately, all the varieties that are sold pitted are invariably bad or tasteless, so for recipes that require pitted or chopped olives you will have to stone them yourself.

Olive oil: With the extraordinary range of fine extra virgin olive oils available now from different countries, and the growing snobbery and mystique that surround this newly fashionable product, it is good to explore the qualities of the different oils for yourself. Like everything else in matters of taste, the best olive oil is the one you like best. And since one olive oil may be good in one context while a different one is good in another, it is worth experimenting.

Oils vary in colour, flavour and aroma depending on the type of tree, the soil in which it grows, whether it grows on a hill or the plain or by the sea, the weather, when and how the olives are harvested, how ripe they are, how quickly the oil is extracted and by what means. The old traditional method is to crush and grind the olives, pits and all, and let the oil rise gradually to the top of the extracted liquid. New methods of production now most commonly used, called 'continuous' methods, separate the liquid from the solid paste, then the oil from the rest of the juice by spinning the paste or liquid at high speed in a drum or centrifuge. The extra virgin oils produced from first cold-pressings by either of these methods are the finest, with the richest flavour and aroma. The bottled varieties can be varietal oils from a single type of olive, or blends. The blending of oils of two or more varieties of different origin with complementary characteristics is an art that usually entails mixing neutral oils with strong-tasting ones to produce a perfect balance. The oils produced by single estates are the most prestigious and expensive, but some of the extra virgin oils produced more cheaply by large commercial operators can be wonderful too. Unfortunately, many of these are lacking in the desirable qualities, and many of the super-expensive oils are hardly worth the expense.

Oils can be light and delicate, or assertive and strong, and their flavours and aromas simple or complex. Flavours range from sweet to pleasantly bitter, through fruity, nutty, spicy and peppery. They can be upfront, or experienced as an aftertaste. Fragrance may be fruity, floral, nutty or grassy, elusive or intense. As with wine, some harvests produce exceptional oil, some more ordinary oils. But blended oils are always the same, as blenders seek to achieve consistency by adjusting their mixes. Their styles reflect local tastes and traditions as well as the preferences – for lightness, for instance – of consumer countries newly converted to olive oil.

You cannot tell the style or quality of an oil by the colour, although a dark green is generally characteristic of a fruity, bitter astringent oil produced from green olives that have not reached maturity, and golden yellow oils are made from sweet ripe black olives late in the season (all olives start green and ripen to black). However, it is not uncommon for green leaves to be crushed with the olives to colour the oil.

In general, the best oils of Provence are light, sweet and fragrant; the oils of Greece are slightly bitter, assertive and hearty; while Portuguese oils are rough and rustic. Spain produces a variety of fruity aromatic oils – Catalan oils have a delicious almondy quality while Andalusian oils have a warm, sweet fruity taste and heady perfume. Italy is famous for the strongly assertive, bitter quality of its Tuscan oils whose peppery aftertaste grates the back of the throat, but the lesser known light, sweet, fruity oils from Liguria, Umbria and the Abruzzi, and the rich, fruity, peppery ones of Apulia, are also very appealing. While all Mediterranean countries produce a certain amount of olive oil, Turkey and Tunisia, where every bit of the countryside is dotted with olive trees, are important producers whose oils are not easily available in Europe. They do not benefit from EU subsidies and cannot afford to promote themselves. Much of the Tunisian product goes to Italy and some to Spain and France to be blended and re-exported. Some of the Italian blends also use Greek and Spanish oils.

Different types of oil are suitable for different dishes. There are no fixed rules, and tastes vary. The best extra virgin oils should be used raw, as a dressing. I like a light, fresh, non-astringent fragrant oil to dress salads, fish and boiled vegetables, and to blend into delicate raw sauces; and a rich, fruity oil for gazpachos and herby green sauces, to dress pasta and drizzle over grilled or fried vegetables, meat or fish. A drop of strong-tasting, bitter, fruity or spicy oil will enhance the taste of a creamy soup, a stew or a tomato sauce and makes a rich dressing for pasta. For deep-frying, use oils labelled 'ordinary virgin olive oil', 'refined olive oil' or simply 'olive oil'. These are produced from second or subsequent pressings, which have then been processed and refined to remove their acidity, and are usually bland.

Some people like to flavour their oil with aromatics such as garlic cloves, chillies, sprigs of basil, rosemary or thyme, bay leaves or fennel seeds. These should be left in the oil for two weeks, then removed, as they may rot.

Pepper: Black pepper, preferably freshly ground, is used throughout the book, unless otherwise stated.

Pomegranate syrup: This is the concentrated syrup or molasses of boiled-down sour pomegranate juice. It is available in Middle Eastern stores.

About Drinks

The traditional spirit of the Mediterranean is flavoured with aniseed – in France it is pastis, distilled from grapes; in the Middle East it is raki, ouzo or zibib; and in Morocco it is mahia, which is made from figs or dates. They are always served with appetizers. Beer and whisky are other warm-weather drinks. In Muslim countries the usual refreshments are pressed lemon, fresh fruit juices, iced syrups and yoghurt beaten with iced water or soda.

In non-Muslim countries wine is always served with meals. It is a habit worth adopting. A simple and robust wine with character and quality, which can stand up to an amalgam of flavours, is what you need. Vinegar and lemon in the accompanying meal will turn a thin dry white flat, and sweetness will make it acid, while spices and chillies will kill a great and complex wine. A young vigorous wine with rough fruit goes well with sour, sweet, spicy and savoury flavours. With a fruity dessert you can serve a sweet wine.

Strong black coffee – Turkish or espresso – is the perfect end to a Mediterranean meal.

About Measures

I have sometimes given numbers of vegetables as well as the weight, only as a rough guide. Bear in mind that sizes vary considerably from one greengrocer and supermarket to another, let alone from one country to another. (I have found, for instance, that in different stores between 5 and 8 'medium' tomatoes weighed 500g.)

The baking dishes I have used are generally round clay ones, but square and rectangular ones will do just as well. The size given is the diameter. I have also used round cake tins.

Mediterranean cooks are not over-concerned with precise measures and prefer to judge by eye if a dish is the right size. They also rely on their taste for adjusting seasonings and aromatics. I would like to encourage you to do the same and trust your good sense, because that really never fails, even if you are dealing with a dish that is new to you.

Salads and Appetizers

Salads and cold vegetable dishes, served as appetizers with drinks, or as side dishes, are some of the most appealing features of Mediterranean eating. They enliven a meal with their traditionally strong flavourings (spices and aromatics are meant to sharpen the appetite) and exuberant colours, and bring variety and excitement to the table. One advantage is that they can be prepared in advance. You can also make a meal out of two or three appetizers accompanied with bread, and perhaps cheese and olives.

Rocket and Tomato Salad | serves 4

This is an Egyptian salad.

> *1 bunch (60g) rocket leaves*
> *3 medium tomatoes, quartered*
> *3 tbsp light extra virgin olive oil*
> *juice of ½ lemon*
> *salt and pepper*
> *about 6 spring onions, sliced*

Cut the rocket leaves into ribbons. Put them in a bowl with the tomato quarters and dress with the remaining ingredients.

Mixed Green Leaf and Herb Salad |

This type of salad became famous long ago as the Provençal *mesclun* and now all our supermarkets sell packs of mixed leaves inspired by it.

> *a mixture of salad leaves (about 200g), such as gem lettuce, oak-leaf lettuce, curly chicory, chicory, watercress, rocket, lamb's lettuce, dandelion and purslane*
> *3–4 tbsp mixed chopped fresh herbs, such as chervil, basil, marjoram, chives, mint, parsley or coriander*
> *Vinaigrette (see page 265)*

Put the salad leaves in a wide shallow bowl and sprinkle on the herbs.

Just before serving, dress the salad lightly with the Vinaigrette.

Variations

Add fried garlic slices or garlic croutons made by rolling small cubes of bread in olive oil flavoured with a little crushed garlic, and toasting them.

Sprinkle with fresh walnut halves.

Purslane Salad with Tomato and Cucumber

serves 4

Purslane is one of the Mediterranean salad leaves that has yet
to be discovered here. You can find the fleshy leaves occasionally, sold in bunches, in Greek and Middle Eastern stores. You
can shred them or leave them whole for this salad, which makes
a light meal.

> 2 bunches (about 250g) purslane
> 4 plum tomatoes, quartered
> 2 small or 1 large cucumber, peeled and cut into thick
>   slices
> 4 spring onions, sliced
> Vinaigrette (see page 265)
> 100g feta cheese, cut into 2cm cubes (optional)
> 8 black olives (optional)

Pull the purslane leaves off the stems. Put them in a bowl with
the rest of the vegetables and dress with the Vinaigrette.

Garnish, if you like, with feta cheese and olives.

Lettuce and Orange Salad | serves 4

Oranges are used in a variety of salads in Morocco, where they use the delicately flavoured argan oil (from the rare argan tree) to dress them. You may like to try sesame or hazelnut oil.

> *1 curly endive or batavia or 2 gem lettuces, cut into ribbons*
> *juice of ½ orange*
> *juice of ½ lemon*
> *½ tbsp orange blossom water*
> *2 tbsp sesame, hazelnut or a light extra virgin olive oil*
> *salt*
> *2 large oranges (sweet or sour), peeled and sliced*

Dress the lettuce with a mixture of the orange and lemon juice, orange blossom water, oil and salt. Scatter in a wide serving dish.

Lay the orange slices on top.

Chopped Cucumber and Mint Salad |

This Middle Eastern cucumber salad is delicately scented and refreshing.

> *1 large cucumber, peeled and grated or chopped in the*
> * food processor*
> *3 tbsp extra virgin olive oil*
> *2 tbsp lemon juice or 1 tbsp white wine vinegar*
> *1 tbsp orange blossom water, or to taste*
> *salt*
> *1 tbsp dried crushed mint leaves*
> *a few black and green olives, to garnish (optional)*

Drain the cucumber. Just before serving, put it into a serving bowl and mix with the rest of the ingredients. Garnish, if you like, with the olives.

White Haricot Bean Salad | serves 4

This is the famous Turkish *piaz*. It makes a snack or light meal.

2 × 400g tins of white haricot beans or cannellini beans
5 tbsp extra virgin olive oil
2 tbsp white wine vinegar
salt and pepper
1 medium mild onion, finely chopped
3 tbsp chopped flat-leafed parsley
10 black olives
2 firm but ripe tomatoes, cut into wedges
2 hard-boiled eggs (large), cut into wedges

Drain the tinned beans, dress with the oil, vinegar, salt and pepper, and mix with the chopped onion and parsley.

Serve garnished with the olives, tomatoes and hard-boiled eggs.

Fennel Salad | serves 4

The delicate anise flavour of fennel is particularly pleasant when it is eaten raw.

> *2 fennel bulbs*
> *Vinaigrette (see page 265)*

Cut the fennel bulbs in slices lengthways. Arrange on a serving plate and pour on the Vinaigrette.

Moroccan Carrot Salad with Yoghurt

This surprisingly soft, creamy salad will do well as an appetizer or side dish.

> *250g (about 2 large) carrots, chopped or grated in the*
>   *food processor*
> *3 tbsp groundnut or light vegetable oil*
> *1 garlic clove, crushed*
> *½ tsp cinnamon*
> *salt*
> *2–3 tbsp lemon juice*
> *150ml plain or thick, strained Greek yoghurt*

Sauté the carrots in the oil with the garlic over low heat, stirring often, for about 10 minutes, until slightly softened but not coloured. Add the cinnamon, salt and lemon juice and cook for about 5 more minutes.

Serve the carrots cold on a flat plate with the yoghurt poured on top.

Spicy Carrot Purée | serves 4

Many North African appetizers are strongly flavoured, usually with cumin, which is meant to whet the appetite.

> *500g (about 4 large) carrots*
> *2 garlic cloves, crushed*
> *1–2 tbsp white wine vinegar*
> *4 tbsp extra virgin olive oil*
> *½ tsp ground cumin or caraway seeds*
> *6 black or green olives*
> *1 Preserved Lemon Peel (see page 267), cut into small*
> *   pieces (optional)*

Boil the carrots in water until soft. Drain and mash them with a fork.

Add the garlic, vinegar, oil and cumin or caraway seeds and mix well. Serve cold, garnished with olives and preserved lemon peel, if using.

Carrot and Sweet Potato Salad | serves 4

North African appetizers can be fiery or, like this one, sweet and delicate.

> *250g (2 large) carrots, cut into 2cm slices*
> *250g (1 large) sweet potato, cut into 2cm cubes*
> *4 tbsp seedless raisins or sultanas*
> *½ tsp powdered ginger*
> *½ tsp cinnamon*
> *salt and pepper*
> *3 tbsp extra virgin olive oil*
> *1 tbsp honey*
> *juice of ½ lemon*

Put the carrots and sweet potato in a pan with just enough water to cover.

Stir in the rest of the ingredients and simmer, uncovered, to reduce the sauce, for about 15 minutes, or until the carrots and sweet potatoes are tender and the sauce is syrupy and thick. Serve cold.

Lentil and Spinach Salad | serves 4

Spinach is paired with every one of the Mediterranean pulses – chick peas, beans, split peas and lentils – in soups, stews and salads. It is one of the age-old combinations that works well. This salad is an old Arab favourite, often accompanied by yoghurt.

200g large brown or green lentils, soaked for 1 hour
salt
1 medium onion, chopped
5–6 tbsp extra virgin olive oil
1 tsp ground coriander
300g spinach
juice of ½–1 lemon
pepper

Drain the lentils and simmer in fresh water for 20 minutes or until tender, adding salt towards the end, then drain.

In a large pan, fry the onion in 2 tbsp of the oil over medium heat until soft. Stir in the coriander.

Wash the spinach and remove the stems only if they are tough. Drain, press all the water out, and put into the pan with the onion. Sprinkle lightly with salt, cover with a lid and let the leaves steam for a moment or two over low heat until they crumple into a soft mass.

Add the drained lentils, lemon juice, some pepper and the remaining oil, and mix well. Serve cold.

Variations

Use frozen leaf spinach. Defrost and add to the fried onion. Sprinkle with salt and cook, stirring, for 5–8 minutes.

Use chick peas or white haricot beans (tinned if you like) instead of the lentils

For a different lentil salad with tomato and cheese, mix the cooked lentils with 3 medium diced ripe tomatoes and 100g mashed feta cheese and dress with Vinaigrette (see page 270).

Courgette Purée | serves 4

In this Moroccan salad with its exotic flavours, the usually bland courgettes are unrecognizable.

> 500g (about 3 large) courgettes
> 1–2 garlic cloves, crushed
> juice of ½ lemon
> 3 tbsp extra virgin olive oil
> ½ tsp ground cumin or caraway seeds
> salt
> pinch of chilli powder
> 100g feta cheese, crumbled with a fork (optional)
> 6 green and black olives (optional)

Boil the courgettes in water until soft. Drain and mash with a fork. Add the garlic, lemon juice, oil, cumin or caraway, salt, and chilli powder, and stir well. Garnish with feta cheese and olives, if you like.

Fried Courgette Slices with Yoghurt serves 4

For this traditional Arab way of serving courgettes, the vegetables may be grilled rather than deep-fried.

> *500g (about 3 large) courgettes, cut into slices lengthways*
> *olive or vegetable oil for frying*
> *salt*
> *400ml plain or strained Greek yoghurt, at room*
> *temperature*

Deep-fry the courgettes in hot oil until they are lightly browned, turning them over once, then drain them on paper towels and sprinkle with salt.

Alternatively, grill them. Arrange the courgette slices on a tray. Brush both sides very lightly with olive oil and sprinkle with salt. Put the tray under the grill and cook the slices, turning them over once, until browned.

Serve hot or cold with the yoghurt poured over.

Variations

The yoghurt may be flavoured with 1 crushed garlic clove and 2tsp dried crushed mint. It should be at room temperature, even when the courgettes are served hot.

Another traditional accompaniment is a Fresh Tomato Sauce (see page 271).

Aubergine slices, cut lengthways, can be prepared in the same way. These are usually salted and left to degorge their juices for 30 minutes before frying, but this step is not obligatory.

Marinated Baby Aubergines | serves 4–6

You find baby aubergines, which are about 10cm long, in Indian and Middle Eastern stores. The dish keeps well for several days.

> 500g baby aubergines
> salt
> 5 garlic cloves, peeled
> 4 tbsp extra virgin olive oil
> 2 tbsp pomegranate syrup (also sold as a molasses or concentrate)
> juice of ½ lemon
> ¼ tsp chilli pepper
> ½ tsp cumin
> 3 tbsp chopped flat-leafed parsley

Wash the baby aubergines, remove the caps but leave the stems. Cut in half lengthways, not right to the end, so that the halves remain attached at the stem end.

Boil in salted water with the garlic cloves for 15 minutes, then drain.

For the marinade, mash the boiled garlic cloves and mix with the rest of the ingredients. Roll the drained aubergines in the marinade, opening them so that the cut sides can absorb it well. Leave for at least half a day and serve cold.

Mashed Aubergine with Pomegranate Syrup

serves 4

This is a Syrian version of the famous aubergine 'caviare' (see variation) which is found all over the Mediterranean. The dark, almost black, pomegranate syrup gives it an exciting sweet-and-sour flavour and intriguing colour. Accompany with warm bread for dipping.

> *about 500g (1 large) aubergine*
> *2 tbsp pomegranate syrup (also sold as a molasses or*
>   *concentrate)*
> *3 tbsp extra virgin olive oil*
> *salt and pepper*
> *1–2 cloves garlic, crushed (optional)*
> *2 tbsp chopped flat-leafed parsley*

Roast and peel the aubergine as described on pages 268. Press the juices out in a colander and chop the flesh finely with two pointed knives (this gives a better texture than blending in a food processor). Do the chopping in the colander, letting the juices escape.

   Put the chopped aubergine in a bowl, add the rest of the ingredients and mix well. Spread the purée on a serving dish, sprinkle with the parsley, and serve.

Variation

For the traditional aubergine 'caviare' add the juice of ½–1 lemon instead of the pomegranate syrup.

Fried Aubergine Slices with Pomegranate Syrup | serves 4

In all Mediterranean countries fried aubergines are common everyday fare. This Syrian version, dressed with pomegranate syrup, is particularly delicious.

> *2 medium aubergines, cut into slices about 1cm thick*
> *salt*
> *olive or vegetable oil for frying*
> *2–3 tbsp pomegranate syrup (also sold as a molasses or concentrate)*
> *3 tbsp water*
> *3 garlic cloves, coarsely chopped*
> *3 tbsp chopped flat-leafed parsley*

Sprinkle the aubergine slices generously with salt, and leave them for 30 minutes to degorge their juices. Then rinse and dry with paper towels.

Deep-fry in about 1.25cm of oil. It should be hot at first, then lower the heat a little, so that the slices do not brown too quickly before they are soft inside. Turn over once. Drain on paper towels and pat gently with more towels on top.

Arrange on a serving dish. Mix the pomegranate syrup with the water and place a little on each aubergine slice.

Fry the garlic very briefly over low heat in 4 tbsp of the frying oil in a small pan, until golden.

Serve cold sprinkled with fried garlic and parsley.

Variations

You can omit the pomegranate syrup and instead serve the fried aubergine slices spread with a layer of thick, strained yoghurt, or tossed in Fresh Tomato Sauce (see page 271).

Pepper and Tomato Appetizer | serves 4

This North African appetizer, called *shoucouka*, can be sweet or peppery hot. Serve it with bread.

2 garlic cloves, finely chopped
2 tbsp extra virgin olive oil
500g (about 6 medium) ripe tomatoes, peeled and
* chopped*
1–2 tsp granulated sugar
salt
½ tsp paprika (optional)
a good pinch of chilli pepper (optional)
3 red and yellow peppers

Fry the garlic in the oil until golden, then add the tomatoes, sugar, salt and the paprika and chilli if using. Cook very gently for 30 minutes or until the sauce is thick and jam-like.

Roast and peel the peppers (for instructions, see page 267–8). Collect the juices that escape and add them to the tomato sauce.

Cut the peeled peppers into small squares and mix with the tomato sauce. Serve cold.

Braised Broad Beans, Peas and Artichokes

serves 4–6

A combination of broad beans and artichokes is found in almost every Mediterranean country. In Sicily green peas are added too. There is something very pleasing about the partnership. This can be served as an appetizer or a side dish.

> 1 medium onion, chopped
> 4 tbsp extra virgin olive oil
> 3 garlic cloves, chopped
> 400g (about 10 small) frozen artichoke hearts or bottoms, sliced or quartered
> 200g shelled green peas or petits pois
> 200g shelled broad beans
> 2 tbsp chopped fresh mint
> 2 tbsp chopped fresh dill
> salt and pepper
> juice of ½ lemon
> 2 tsp granulated sugar
> about 4 tbsp water

Fry the onion in the oil until golden

Add the garlic, artichokes, peas and beans, and sauté gently, stirring, for about 2 minutes.

Add the mint and dill, salt, pepper, lemon juice and sugar, and moisten with the water. Cook with the lid on for 10 minutes or until the vegetables are tender, adding a little water if necessary.

Serve hot or cold.

Note

To prepare and use fresh artichoke hearts, see page 269.

Tip

It is difficult in this country to find baby artichokes that you can eat whole and it is a big effort to trim the usual artichokes to obtain the hearts. I use frozen artichoke hearts or bottoms (tinned ones are not much good). You can now get podded broad beans and peas at a few supermarkets. At an Iranian store near my house where I get my frozen artichoke bottoms (from Egypt in packs of 400g) I recently also found very good frozen skinned broad beans.

Mushrooms with Garlic and White Wine

serves 4

This is a traditional way of cooking mushrooms in France and Italy. A mixture of wild mushrooms including boletus, chanterelles and morels makes a splendid but very expensive dish. Shiitakes are a very good alternative. Serve them, if you like, with toasted brioche halves or slices.

> *500g shiitake mushrooms or a mixture of other varieties*
> *1 medium onion, chopped*
> *3 tbsp extra virgin olive oil*
> *3 garlic cloves, chopped*
> *juice of ½ lemon*
> *150ml fruity dry white wine*
> *salt and pepper*
> *3 tbsp chopped flat-leafed parsley*

Clean the mushrooms and cut very large ones into 2.5cm pieces.

Sauté the onion lightly in the oil until soft. Add the mushrooms and garlic and cook until almost all their juices have evaporated. Add the lemon juice and the white wine, season with salt and pepper, and cook for a further 5–10 minutes.

Stir in the parsley and serve hot or cold.

Sweet Potato Salad | serves 4

In this Moroccan salad, the curious mix of sweet and spicy is quite delicious. It is nice as it is but you may add, if you like, a handful of black olives, chopped Preserved Lemon Peel (see page 272) and a tablespoon of capers.

> 1 large onion, chopped
> 5 tbsp extra virgin olive oil
> 750g sweet potatoes, cut into 4cm cubes
> ½–¾ tsp ground (powdered) ginger
> pinch of saffron powder (optional)
> 1 tsp paprika
> 1 tsp cinnamon
> pinch of cayenne, to taste
> juice of ½–1 lemon
> 2 tsp granulated sugar
> salt
> 4 tbsp chopped coriander or flat-leafed parsley

In a saucepan, fry the onion in 3 tbsp of the oil until soft. Add the sweet potatoes and just enough water to cover.

Stir in the ginger, saffron, if using, paprika, cinnamon, cayenne, lemon juice, sugar and salt. Cook, uncovered, for 15 minutes or until the sweet potatoes are tender, turning the potatoes over once; be careful not to let them overcook and fall apart.

The sauce should be much reduced to a thick, syrupy consistency. If it is not, transfer the potatoes with a slotted spoon to a serving dish and reduce the sauce further by boiling. Just before the end of cooking, stir in the coriander or parsley and the remaining oil. Serve cold.

Mashed Potato Salad with Anchovies | serves 4–6

This Tunisian salad can be served as an appetizer or side salad and goes well with fish. The anchovies are optional.

> *750g potatoes*
> *salt*
> *4 tbsp extra virgin olive oil*
> *1½ tbsp white wine vinegar*
> *pepper*
> *½ tsp Harissa (see page 268) or a good pinch of cayenne (optional)*
> *50g (1 small tin) anchovy fillets, finely chopped (optional)*
> *1–3 garlic cloves, crushed (optional)*
> *a good bunch parsley, finely chopped*
> *2 tbsp capers, squeezed to get rid of excess vinegar*

Peel and boil the potatoes in lightly salted water until soft, then drain, keeping a little of the cooking water.

Mash the potatoes with the oil and vinegar and 2–4 tbsp of the cooking water until they have a soft, moist texture. Add the rest of the ingredients and mix well. Serve cold.

Spicy Walnut Paste | serves 6–8

This delicious Turkish relish, called *muhammara*, can be served as a dip with bread or to accompany a salad. It keeps very well for several days, so you can make a large batch.

> *150g shelled walnuts*
> *1½–2 tbsp tomato purée*
> *1 slice wholemeal bread, crusts removed and lightly toasted*
> *8 tbsp extra virgin olive oil*
> *2 tbsp pomegranate syrup or the juice of ½ lemon*
> *1 tsp coarsely ground hot red chilli flakes or a pinch of chilli powder*
> *1 tsp cumin*
> *2 tsp granulated sugar*
> *salt*

Blend everything together to a paste in the food processor.

Bulgur Salad with Walnuts | serves 4–6

In this scrumptious and nutritious Turkish salad, called *batrik*, bulgur is soaked in the juice of fresh puréed tomatoes and is enriched with walnuts, pistachios and onions. It can be made mild or hot with chilli pepper.

>   *150g fine- or medium-ground bulgur*
>   *500g (about 6 medium) tomatoes, peeled and puréed in a*
>   *food processor*
>   *juice of ½ lemon*
>   *1 tsp tomato purée*
>   *3–4 tbsp extra virgin olive oil*
>   *salt*
>   *a pinch or more chilli flakes or chilli powder, to taste*
>   *1 small mild onion or 5 spring onions, finely chopped*
>   *100g walnuts or pistachios, or a mixture of the two*

Mix the bulgur with the blended tomatoes, lemon juice and tomato purée, and leave for an hour or until the grain has absorbed the juice and become tender. Add the oil, salt and chilli flakes or powder to taste. Just before serving add the onion and walnuts or pistachios.

Couscous Salad | serves 4–6

I have not come across a couscous salad in North Africa, but France is awash with what they call *taboulé* (the name of the Lebanese bulgur, mint and parsley salad).

> 250g medium couscous
> 1 green or red pepper, diced
> 3 medium tomatoes, peeled and diced
> 10 spring onions, thinly sliced
> salt and pepper
> juice of 1 lemon, or more, to taste
> 5–8 tbsp extra virgin olive oil
> a few sprigs of fresh mint, shredded
> a large bunch flat-leafed parsley, chopped

Put the couscous in a bowl, add 300ml cold water and mix well. Leave for at least 30 minutes. When the grain is swollen and tender, mix in the rest of the ingredients.

Brown Lentils and Rice with Caramelized Onions | serves 4–6

In Syria and Lebanon this dish is called *mudardara*. In Egypt, it is known as *megadarra*. It is eaten cold or warm, usually accompanied by yoghurt and a cucumber and tomato salad. I have featured it before in my books but it is such a classic that it should be included here too. American long-grain rice does not need washing but basmati rice does. Pour boiling water over it, stir and leave for a few minutes, then rinse in cold water in a sieve.

> *2 large onions*
> *125ml light extra virgin olive oil*
> *150g large brown lentils, soaked in cold water for 1 hour*
> *700ml water*
> *½ tsp cinnamon*
> *½ tsp allspice*
> *150g American long-grain or Basmati rice*
> *salt and plenty of pepper*

Prepare the garnish first. Slice 1½ onions into half-moons and fry in 3 tbsp of the oil, over medium heat, stirring frequently, until they are very dark brown and almost caramelized. Set aside.

Chop the remaining onion and fry in 1 tbsp of the oil over medium heat until soft and golden.

Drain and simmer the lentils in the water with the cinnamon and allspice for about 15 minutes.

Add the rice and a pinch of salt and simmer, covered, for 18 minutes or until the rice is just tender.

Mix the lentils and rice with the fried chopped onion and the remaining oil. Season with salt and pepper.

Serve warm or cold with the caramelized onions sprinkled on top.

Variation

Another method, which might be easier, is to boil the lentils and the rice in separate pans, then drain and mix together when each is done.

Root Vegetables in Olive Oil | serves 4–6

Vegetables cooked together in a mixture of olive oil and water with herbs, and served cold, are a speciality of the Eastern Mediterranean. This winter selection has a wonderful taste and texture.

> *2 large carrots, cut into 2cm slices*
> *450g (1 medium) celeriac, peeled and cut into 2cm cubes*
> *250g (1 medium) sweet potato, peeled and cut into 2cm cubes*
> *6 tbsp light extra virgin olive oil*
> *juice of ½ lemon*
> *salt and pepper*
> *1–2 tsp granulated sugar*
> *2 tbsp chopped fresh dill*

Put the vegetables in a large pan with the oil and sauté over low heat, turning them occasionally, for 5 minutes.

Add the lemon juice, salt, pepper and sugar to taste and just enough water to cover. Simmer for 25–30 minutes or until the vegetables are very tender. (Cover and cook for the first 20 minutes, then uncover and simmer to reduce the sauce.)

Add the dill towards the end. Serve cold.

Soups

Soups are always a pleasant way to start a meal but, accompanied with a good slice of bread, a soup can also be served as a main course or as a meal in itself. In the Mediterranean, soups range from light vegetable creams and iced summer soups to aromatic broths with vegetables and rice, and rich and substantial winter combinations with lentils, beans and chick peas.

Chilled Melon Soup | serves 4

This delicately flavoured, refreshing summer soup is thickened in the traditional Mediterranean way, with ground almonds. Choose sweet ripe melons.

1.5kg (1–2) melons, to yield about 1kg flesh
2.5cm piece of ginger, grated (or use its juice, squeezed out using a garlic press)
1½–2 tbsp white wine vinegar, or to taste
2 tbsp extra virgin olive oil
salt and white pepper
6 tbsp ground almonds

Cut away the peel and rind and remove the seeds of the melon or melons.

In a blender or food processor, liquidize the flesh with the rest of the ingredients, then chill in the refrigerator. The soup will thicken to a creamy consistency when the almonds absorb the juice.

Serve cold.

Green Vegetable Soup with Lemon serves 6–8

This is one of my favourite soups that our family had in Egypt. It is very lemony (its name, *hamud*, means 'lemony' in Arabic) and also minty. We made it with chicken stock, but vegetable stock made with stock cubes will do. Cooked rice is added at the end, which makes it a substantial dish. Add the lemon to taste; you might not like it too sharp.

> 2 litres vegetable stock made with 2½ cubes
> 2–3 medium leeks, cut into 2cm slices
> 1 medium head of celery with leaves, cut into 2cm slices
> 1 large potato, peeled and diced
> salt and white pepper
> 3 large garlic cloves, chopped
> juice of 1–3 lemons, to taste
> 1 tsp granulated sugar, or more to taste
> 3 medium courgettes, cut into 1.25cm slices
> 6 artichoke hearts (for preparation, see page 264), cut in
>   half – you may use frozen ones (optional)
> 100g pine nuts or blanched almonds, ground in a food
>   processor
> 2 tbsp dried mint
> 200g American long-grain rice, cooked (weight uncooked)

In a large pan bring the stock to the boil. Add the leeks, celery and potato. Add salt and pepper, and the garlic, lemon juice and sugar, and simmer for 30 minutes.

Add the courgettes and artichokes, if using, and simmer for another 15 minutes. Add the pine nuts or almonds (the pine nuts give a particularly fine flavour), and mint, and cook for another 5–10 minutes. It is important at this point to taste and adjust the flavourings.

Serve in soup bowls over the hot rice.

Red Gazpacho | serves 6 or more

There are many versions of the famous Andalusian cold soup. This thick, bright red tomato version, with no added water and a generous garnish, is my favourite. It is quite the best thing you could want to eat on a hot summer's day.

1 red pepper, cut into pieces
1–3 garlic cloves, crushed
3 slices of white bread, crusts removed and cut into pieces
1.5kg ripe plum tomatoes, peeled
6 tbsp sherry or white wine vinegar
5 tbsp extra virgin olive oil
salt and pepper
1–2 tsp granulated sugar, or to taste

For the garnish
12 ice cubes
1 medium cucumber, peeled and finely diced
1 red onion or 4 spring onions, chopped
1 green pepper, finely diced

Purée the pepper in a food processor. Add the rest of the soup ingredients and blend to a light smooth cream, adding a little cold water, if necessary, to thin it. Chill, covered, in the refrigerator.

Serve, adding 2 ice cubes to each soup bowl, accompanied by the garnish ingredients each on a separate little plate.

Pumpkin Soup with Milk | serves 4

There are pumpkin soups in every country around the Mediterranean. This lovely one is from Provence. You can usually get orange-fleshed pumpkins in Indian and Middle Eastern stores throughout the year. Because the taste of pumpkin varies, it is important to get the right balance of salt and sugar. Start with a little of each, then taste, and add more if necessary.

> *a 750g piece of orange pumpkin (weighed with the seeds and fibres removed)*
> *500g (about 2 large) potatoes, peeled and cubed*
> *1.25 litres milk*
> *salt and white pepper*
> *1 tbsp granulated sugar, or to taste*
> *2 bay leaves*
> *1 sprig of thyme*
> *2 cinnamon sticks*
> *150ml crème fraiche, sour cream or thick, strained yoghurt*

Peel the pumpkin and cut the pulp into cubes. Put it in a pan with the potatoes and milk, a little salt, pepper and sugar, the bay leaves, thyme and cinnamon sticks.

Simmer, covered, on low heat, for 20–25 minutes or until the potatoes and pumpkin are very soft.

Remove the bay leaves, thyme and cinnamon sticks and mash the vegetables with a potato masher. Adjust the seasoning and add water to thin the soup, if necessary. Cook for a further 1 or 2 minutes.

Serve hot, garnished with a dollop of crème fraiche, sour cream or yoghurt, or let people help themselves.

Mushroom Soup | serves 4

This soup, thickened with potato rather than flour, has a wonderful fresh taste.

> *500g (about 2 large) potatoes*
> *1.5 litres water or vegetable stock (you may use a stock cube)*
> *250ml fruity dry white wine (optional)*
> *250g shiitake mushrooms*
> *2 garlic cloves, crushed*
> *4 tbsp light vegetable oil*
> *salt and pepper*
> *a large bunch flat-leafed parsley, finely chopped*
> *1 lemon, cut into wedges*
> *150ml crème fraiche (optional)*

Peel the potatoes and cut them into pieces. Put them in a pan with the water or stock and the wine, if using, and simmer until the potatoes are soft. Then crush them with a potato masher.

Chop the mushrooms in a food processor. In a frying pan, sauté the mushrooms and garlic in the oil for 5 minutes, stirring constantly. Pour into the pan with the crushed potatoes.

Add salt and pepper and simmer for a few minutes. Just before serving, add the parsley and heat through. Serve accompanied with lemon wedges and, if you like, crème fraiche.

Spinach and Yoghurt Soup | serves 4

You find many different yoghurt soups in the Eastern Mediterranean. This hot version is exquisite.

> *350g spinach or frozen leaf spinach*
> *1 medium onion, chopped*
> *3 spring onions, finely chopped*
> *2 tbsp sunflower or vegetable oil*
> *100g American long-grain rice*
> *750ml water*
> *¼ tsp turmeric (optional)*
> *salt and white pepper*
> *500ml yoghurt*
> *1 garlic clove, crushed*

Wash the spinach and remove the stems only if they are thick and hard. Defrost if using frozen spinach. Drain and cut into strips.

In a large saucepan, fry the onion and spring onions in the oil until soft.

Add the rice and stir to coat it with oil. Pour in the water, add the turmeric, if using, season with salt and pepper and simmer for 15 minutes.

Add the spinach and cook for 5 minutes or until it softens and the rice is tender. The rice should not be too soft and mushy.

Beat the yoghurt with the garlic, then beat it into the soup. Heat through but do not boil or the yoghurt will curdle. Serve at once.

Red Lentil Soup | serves 4

There are several versions of this popular Middle Eastern soup. The flavouring here is rather delicate, but you can make it more spicy by following the variation.

> 1 medium onion, chopped
> 1 small carrot, finely chopped
> a bunch of celery leaves, chopped
> 4 tbsp sunflower or vegetable oil
> 200g split red lentils
> 1 litre vegetable stock (you may use 1 stock cube)
> salt and pepper
> ¾–1 tsp cumin
> juice of ½ lemon
> 1 large onion, cut in half then sliced

Soften the chopped onion, carrot and celery leaves in 2 tbsp of the oil in a large saucepan.

Add the lentils, stock, salt and pepper and simmer for 30–45 minutes, until the lentils have disintegrated. Add water if the soup needs thinning and stir in the cumin and lemon juice.

Meanwhile, fry the sliced onion in the remaining oil over medium-high heat, stirring often until crisp and very brown – almost caramelized.

Serve the soup hot. Garnish each serving with a scattering of fried onions.

Variation

Before serving, stir in 4 chopped garlic cloves fried in 2 tbsp olive oil with 1 tsp ground coriander and 2 tsp dried crushed mint. A pinch of chilli pepper may be added too.

Cream of Bean and Barley Soup | serves 6

This deliciously creamy and satisfying soup is from Italy.

> *125g pearl barley*
> *1.5 litres water, or more*
> *1 medium onion, quartered*
> *1 medium carrot, cut into thick slices*
> *1 celery stalk, cut into thick slices*
> *2 garlic cloves, peeled*
> *salt and pepper*
> *400g tin white haricot or cannellini beans*
> *2 lemons, quartered*
> *extra virgin olive oil*

Put the barley in a pan with 1 litre of the water. Bring to the boil and skim the surface.

Add the onion, carrot, celery and garlic and simmer for 1 hour or until the barley is very soft, adding more water if it becomes too dry. Season with salt and pepper to taste.

Pour the soup in batches into the food processor with the drained beans and enough water to obtain a creamy soup. Blend to a cream, adding more water if necessary. Return to the pan to heat through.

Serve hot with the quartered lemons and pass around a bottle of olive oil to drizzle into the soup.

Chick Pea and Lentil Soup | serves 8–10

This rich and filling winter soup is the Moroccan *harira*. It tastes just as good the day after it's made.

> *250g chick peas, soaked in water for at least 1 hour or overnight*
> *3 litres water*
> *1 large onion, coarsely chopped*
> *400g tin chopped tomatoes*
> *3 celery stalks and leaves, sliced*
> *2 tbsp tomato purée*
> *pepper*
> *½–¾ tsp ground ginger*
> *1 tsp cinnamon*
> *200g large brown or green lentils, soaked for 1 hour then drained*
> *salt*
> *juice of ½ lemon*
> *500g (about 4) courgettes, sliced*
> *100g vermicelli, broken into bits by crushing in your hands*
> *a large bunch flat-leafed parsley, coarsely chopped*
> *a large bunch coriander, coarsely chopped*

Drain the chick peas and put them in a large pan with the water, onion, tomatoes, celery, and tomato purée. Add pepper and simmer, covered, for 1 hour or until the chick peas are very tender.

Add the ginger, cinnamon and lentils and cook for 20 minutes, or until the lentils are soft. Add salt to taste.

Add the lemon juice, courgettes and vermicelli, and more water if necessary, and cook for 10 more minutes. Just before serving, add the parsley and coriander.

Pies and Tarts

Pies and tarts are perfect buffet food and make ideal main dishes for dinner parties. The Eastern Mediterranean specializes in pies made with filo pastry, filled with cheese or spinach, or, more unusually, with mashed aubergine or pumpkin. The Western Mediterranean is justly renowned for its open vegetable tarts, some of the most delightful of which are to be found in the South of France.

Filo Rolls | to make 2 filo rolls to serve 4

A filo pie accompanied by a salad makes an attractive meal. There are dozens of traditional pies made with filo, with different shapes, sizes and fillings, in all the countries that were once part of the Ottoman Empire.

One of the easiest shapes to prepare is a roll that can be cut into portions at the table. Fill it with one of the fillings given on the following pages.

> *1 recipe filling (choose one of those given on pages 75–9)*
> *4 sheets of filo*
> *3 tbsp melted butter or vegetable oil*
> *1 large egg yolk, mixed with 1 tsp water*
> *2–4 tbsp sesame seeds to sprinkle (optional)*

Pre-heat the oven to 180°C/350°F/Gas 4.

Prepare one of the fillings and be ready to work fast with the filo. Take out one sheet and lightly brush with melted butter or oil. Place another sheet on top and brush with melted butter or oil.

Spoon half the filling in a fat line along one long edge, about 2.5cm from the edge and 4cm from the two ends. Lift the edge over the filling and very carefully roll up into a long thin roll, folding the ends in midway so that the filling does not ooze out. You must do this quickly because the filling is moist and if it lies too long on the filo, the pastry will be too wet to handle.

Placing the sheets on a tea towel and lifting the towel makes it easier.

Brush the top of the roll with egg yolk and water mixture and, if you wish, sprinkle with sesame seeds. Repeat the whole process with the next two sheets of filo.

Bake for 45 minutes or until crisp and brown.

Tip

There may be problems with the frozen commercial filo. Too often the sheets are stuck together and tear when you try to separate them. A few brands are invariably good, so when you find a good one, keep to it. You can also get the fresh variety in Greek and Middle Eastern bakeries and groceries. If using frozen filo, defrost 3 hours before you are ready to use it.

Spinach Filling | fills 2 rolls to serve 4

> *500g fresh or frozen whole leaf spinach*
> *100g cottage cheese*
> *100g feta cheese, mashed*
> *2 large eggs, lightly beaten*
> *salt, if necessary, and pepper*
> *a good pinch of nutmeg*

Wash the fresh spinach, remove the stems only if they are tough, and drain.

Put the leaves in a large pan, cover, and cook over low heat for a few minutes only, until they crumple into a soft mass. Drain and press as much of the water out as you can. If using frozen spinach simply thaw and squeeze all the water out with your hands. If there is liquid, the pastry will become soggy and tear.

Combine the spinach with the rest of the filling ingredients. When adding salt, take into consideration the saltiness of the feta cheese.

Mushroom Filling | fills 2 rolls to serve 4

This is an Italian filling used for cannelloni but it also makes a good filling for a filo roll.

> *500g mushrooms, sliced*
> *4 tbsp vegetable oil or light extra virgin olive oil*
> *3 garlic cloves, crushed*
> *salt and pepper*
> *4 tbsp flat-leafed parsley, chopped*
> *125g ricotta*

Sauté the mushrooms briefly in the oil with the garlic until tender, adding salt and pepper. Finish over high heat to reduce the juices. The mushrooms should be almost dry.

Add the parsley and allow to cool, then mix with the ricotta.

Cheese Filling | fills 2 rolls to serve 4–8

Filo rolls filled with this mild-tasting cheese mixture can be served as a main course or as a tea-time savoury.

125g Edam, grated
125g Gouda, grated
125g Cheddar, grated
125g cottage cheese
2 large eggs, lightly beaten
pepper to taste

Put all the ingredients in a food processor and blend to a homogenous paste.

Variations

Add 3 tbsp finely chopped dill or mint and ¼ tsp nutmeg to the filling.

Alternative fillings are cottage cheese and feta, or these two with Gruyère.

Aubergine Purée Filling | fills 2 rolls to serve 4

> *750g aubergines*
> *125g Gruyère, grated*
> *white pepper*
> *¼ tsp nutmeg (optional)*
> *2 large eggs, lightly beaten*

Prick the aubergines with a knife in a few places and roast them in a 250°C/480°F/Gas10 oven for 30 minutes, turning them once. Or put them under the grill for 15–20 minutes and turn them until the flesh feels soft and the skin is blackened.

Peel. In a colander chop the flesh, letting the juices drain out. Then mash with a fork, still in the colander, and mix with the rest of the filling ingredients.

Pumpkin Filling | fills 2 rolls to serve 4

1kg slice of orange pumpkin, cut into pieces
125ml water
100g freshly grated Parmesan cheese
2 tsp granulated sugar
salt to taste
2 large eggs, lightly beaten

Put the pumpkin in a pan with the water and steam, with the lid on, for 15–20 minutes, or until the pumpkin is very soft. Drain, return to the pan, and mash with a potato masher or a fork. Cook over a low heat to dry the paste out, stirring with a wooden spoon.

Mix with the rest of the ingredients. When adding salt, take into consideration the saltiness of the cheese.

Creamy Cheese Bake with Filo Pastry | serves 4

In this version of the Turkish *sutlu borek*, filo pastry is baked in a light creamy custard and becomes soft, like sheets of ever-so-thin pasta. Accompanied with a salad, it makes a scrumptious, homely meal.

> *150g feta cheese*
> *150g cottage cheese*
> *3 large eggs*
> *3 tbsp chopped flat-leafed parsley*
> *125g/5 sheets filo*
> *25g/2 tbsp unsalted butter, melted*
> *300ml milk*

Pre-heat the oven to 180°C/350°F/Gas 4.

To prepare the filling, mash the feta with a fork and mix with the cottage cheese, 1 egg and the parsley.

Open out the sheets of filo, leaving them in a pile. Brush the top one lightly with melted butter and fit it, buttered side up, into a greased round baking dish about 30cm in diameter, bringing the sheet up the sides and folding it. Fit the second sheet over it and brush lightly with butter.

Spread the filling evenly over the pastry. Cover with the remaining sheets, brushing each with melted butter and folding them. Fold the top one so that it presents a smooth surface and brush with butter.

Bake for 15 minutes until lightly coloured, then remove from the oven.

Lightly beat the remaining 2 eggs with the milk and pour over the hot pie (you do not need to add salt because the feta cheese is very salty). Return to the oven and bake for about 30 minutes or until the custard is absorbed and set and the top of the pastry is golden.

Serve hot, cut into wedges.

Savoury Shortcrust Pastry

enough for a 28cm tart to serve 6

This classic shortcrust pastry works well with all kinds of fillings.

> *125g unsalted butter*
> *250g plain flour*
> *¼ tsp salt*
> *1 large egg, lightly beaten*
> *1–2 tbsp milk (if required)*
> *1 large egg white, to glaze (optional)*

Pre-heat the oven to 180°C/350°F/Gas 4.

Cut the butter into small pieces and rub it into the flour and salt with your hands until it becomes like damp sand in texture.

Add the egg, mix well, and work very briefly with your hand until the dough holds together in a soft ball, adding a little milk if necessary. Cover in cling film and leave in a cool place for 1 hour.

Grease a 28cm pie pan, a tart pan with a removable bottom, or flan mould, and line the bottom and sides with the dough by pressing it in with the palms of your hands (with this soft dough, it is easier to do this than to roll it out).

To bake the crust blind before putting in the filling, prick the bottom in a few places with a fork, brush with egg white and bake for 10–15 minutes. Remove from the oven and let it cool. Pour in the filling mixture and bake for 30 minutes or longer, depending on the filling.

Cheese and Fennel Tart | serves 6–8

The combination of cheese with the delicate flavour of fennel makes a lovely filling.

> *1 recipe Savoury Shortcrust Pastry (see page 82)*
> *1 large egg white*
> *1 large or 2 small fennel bulbs, quartered and sliced*
> *salt*
> *2 large eggs, lightly beaten*
> *125ml double cream*
> *125ml milk*
> *100g Gruyère, Emmental or Fontina cheese, grated*
> *pepper*
> *pinch of nutmeg*

Pre-heat the oven to 200°C/400°F/Gas6.

Prepare the pastry shell. Brush it with egg white, prick it all over with a fork, and bake it blind for 10 minutes. Let it cool.

Boil the fennel slices in salted water until they soften, then drain.

Beat the eggs with the cream and milk and mix in the cheese, pepper, a little salt (taking into account the saltiness of the cheese) and nutmeg.

Spread the drained fennel pieces over the bottom of the cooled pastry shell, and pour the cheese mixture on top.

Bake for 30 minutes and serve hot.

Variation

Instead of fennel, use 6–8 celery stalks.

Mushroom Tart | serves 6

The mushrooms in this tart are given a delicate wine flavour.
I use shiitake mushrooms, but you may use wild mushrooms
such as ceps and morels if you prefer.

> *1 recipe Savoury Shortcrust Pastry (see page 82)*
> *1 large egg white*
> *500g shiitake mushrooms*
> *4 tbsp extra virgin olive oil*
> *125ml fruity dry white wine*
> *salt and pepper*
> *4 large eggs, lightly beaten*
> *200ml single cream*
> *pinch of nutmeg*

Pre-heat the oven to 180°C/350°F/Gas 4.

Make the shortcrust pastry and leave in a cool place for
about 1 hour, then roll out and line a 30cm flan mould or pie
pan, pressing it up the sides.

Brush the pastry top with egg white and bake it blind for
15 minutes. Let it cool.

For the filling (start when the dough is resting), wash and
drain the mushrooms. Trim the root ends if necessary. Leave
them whole or cut in half if too large. Heat the oil in a large
pan over medium heat, add the mushrooms and sauté for
2 minutes, stirring and turning them over. Add the wine, salt

and pepper and cook for about 10 minutes, until the mush-rooms are tender, turning them over gently.

Beat the eggs with the cream and the strained juices from the mushrooms, which together with the reduced wine should amount to 200ml. Add more salt and pepper to taste and a touch of nutmeg. Arrange the mushrooms in the cooled pastry case with their tops showing. Pour the flan mixture over them and bake for 45 minutes or until the cream has set.

Serve hot.

Tomato Tart | serves 4

This is a beautiful tart, exquisite and fresh tasting, and very simple to make.

> *250g bought puff pastry, defrosted*
> *1 large egg white*
> *1 large onion, finely chopped*
> *4 tbsp extra virgin olive oil*
> *2 garlic cloves, finely chopped*
> *salt and pepper*
> *5 ripe but firm plum tomatoes, cut into 0.5cm slices*
> *½–1 tsp granulated sugar*
> *12 basil leaves, shredded*

Pre-heat the oven to 230°C/450°F/Gas 8.

Roll out the puff pastry into a round to fit into a 30cm tart dish. (This pastry shrinks quite a bit and will turn out much smaller when it is baked, even if you let it hang over the sides.) Put it in the refrigerator for 30 minutes.

Brush the pastry case with half the egg white (this prevents it from getting too soggy with juice), prick the bottom all over with a fork (so that it puffs up evenly), and bake it blind in the hot oven for 10 minutes or until it puffs up and is golden. Take it out, turn it over, brush the other side with the remaining egg white and return it to the oven for another 8 minutes or until this side is crisp and brown. Let it cool.

Fry the onion in 2 tbsp of the oil until soft. Add the garlic and fry, stirring until golden. Remove from the heat. Allow to cool then spread a layer all over the baked pastry case. Sprinkle very lightly with salt and pepper.

Arrange the tomato slices on top of the onions, so that they overlap in circles. Brush with the remaining olive oil and sprinkle lightly with salt, pepper and sugar.

Place the filled tart in the oven and bake for 15–20 minutes. Serve sprinkled with the shredded basil leaves.

Variation

You may use 500g cherry tomatoes cut in half and arranged with the cut sides up.

Pasta

A century and a half ago, the foods of Bologna – the pastas with meat sauces in particular – came to represent the ideal Italian cuisine. Pellegrino Artusi, the author of Italy's most famous cookery book, *La scienza in cucina e l'arte di mangiare bene* (Science in the kitchen and the art of eating well), published in 1891, told his readers to 'take a bow when you meet Bolognese cooking'. Even in the fifties and sixties Bolognese cooks were still winning all the prizes, but these days it is the vegetable and seafood pastas of southern Italy and Sicily that are fashionable.

Pasta and Mushrooms | serves 4

Wild mushrooms make this a royal dish but are costly. Shiitake mushrooms are a good alternative.

> *500g shiitake mushrooms, or a mixture of wild*
> *mushrooms*
> *1 medium onion, chopped*
> *3 tbsp extra virgin olive oil*
> *1 garlic clove, finely chopped*
> *juice of ½ lemon*
> *150ml dry white wine*
> *a few sprigs of marjoram, chopped*
> *salt and pepper*
> *250ml double cream*
> *400g tagliatelle or taglierini*

Wash the mushrooms and trim the root ends if necessary. Cut very large ones into 2.5cm pieces.

Sauté the onion lightly in the oil over medium heat. Add the mushrooms and garlic and cook until nearly dry. Add the lemon juice and white wine, marjoram, salt and pepper and cook for 2 minutes. Add the cream, and cook until the sauce is thick.

Cook the pasta in boiling salted water until al dente, drain and serve at once with the sauce spooned on top.

Pasta with Peas, Broad Beans and Artichokes

serves 4

1 medium onion, chopped
4 tbsp olive oil
½ gem lettuce, shredded
125ml vegetable stock or white wine
500g fresh shelled or frozen petits pois, defrosted
500g fresh shelled or frozen broad beans, defrosted
2 tsp dried crushed mint
salt and pepper
4 frozen artichoke hearts or bottoms, quartered
400g pasta
grated Parmesan cheese

Fry the onion in 2 tbsp of the oil until soft. Add the gem lettuce and sauté until it wilts.

Add the stock or white wine, the peas and beans and the mint. Season with salt and pepper and simmer for a few minutes until the vegetables are just tender. Add the artichokes and heat through.

Cook the pasta in boiling salted water until al dente, drain and mix with the remaining oil. Serve with the sauce poured over, accompanied with the Parmesan.

Spaghetti with Peppers and Aubergines

serves 4

This Sicilian pasta is called *Vesuvio* because the colours resemble the lava boiling out of the volcano.

> 1 large aubergine, cut into 2cm cubes
> salt
> 2 peppers, yellow or red
> olive oil
> 3 garlic cloves, peeled and chopped
> 500g (about 6 medium) tomatoes, peeled and coarsely
>   chopped
> pepper
> 1½ tsp granulated sugar
> 400g spaghetti
> 8 black olives, pitted and chopped
> 1 tbsp capers, squeezed of their vinegar
> 3 tbsp shredded or torn basil leaves
> grated pecorino (Romano) or Parmesan cheese (optional)

Sprinkle the aubergine with salt and leave for 1 hour, then rinse and dry in a cloth.

Roast the peppers (for directions see page 263). When cool enough to handle, peel and deseed them and cut them into ribbons.

Fry the aubergine cubes in hot oil briefly until tender and

lightly browned, turning them over once, then drain on paper towels.

In a large pan, fry the garlic in 2 tbsp of oil until it begins to colour. Add the tomatoes, season with salt, pepper and sugar and simmer for 15 minutes.

Boil the spaghetti in plenty of salted water until al dente, then drain.

Just before you are ready to serve, add the olives and capers, the aubergine, peppers and the basil to the tomato sauce, and heat through. Pour over the pasta.

Serve with pecorino (Romano) or Parmesan cheese, if you like.

Green Linguine with Spinach and Pine Nuts

serves 4

This is beautiful to look at and delightful to eat.

> *500g fresh spinach or frozen whole leaf spinach,*
>   *defrosted*
> *2 garlic cloves, chopped or crushed*
> *2 tbsp sunflower oil*
> *salt and pepper*
> *175ml double cream*
> *3–4 tbsp pine nuts, raw or toasted*
> *400g green linguine*
> *salt*
> *50g butter, cut into pieces*
> *grated Parmesan or pecorino (Romano) cheese*

Wash and drain the spinach. Remove the stems only if they are tough. If using frozen spinach, defrost.

In a very large pan over medium heat, sauté the garlic lightly in the oil until golden, then add the fresh spinach. Put the lid on and let the spinach cook by steaming in the water that clings to it, stirring occasionally. As soon as it crumples into a soft mass – it does so very quickly – remove from the heat. (Frozen spinach needs only a few minutes' cooking.)

Season with salt and pepper, and stir in the cream and pine nuts.

Drop the linguine into plenty of vigorously boiling salted water and cook until al dente. Drain and serve mixed with the butter and topped with the spinach sauce.

Accompany with the grated cheese.

Spaghetti with Herbs and Roasted Cherry Tomatoes | serves 4

750g cherry tomatoes, cut in half
salt
3–4 garlic cloves, chopped
1–1½ small hot red chilli peppers, deseeded and chopped
  (optional)
125ml extra virgin olive oil
4 sun-dried tomatoes, finely sliced (optional)
a large bunch mixed fresh herbs, such as basil, marjoram,
  oregano, mint, chervil, chives and tarragon, chopped
400g spaghetti or other pasta
grated pecorino (Romano) or Parmesan cheese

Cook the tomatoes, cut side up, under the grill, until they soften slightly, and sprinkle very lightly with salt.

For the sauce, fry the garlic and chilli peppers in 2 tbsp of the oil until the aroma rises, then remove from the heat. Mix with the remaining oil, the sun-dried tomatoes, if using, and the herbs.

Cook the pasta in boiling salted water until al dente and drain. Mix with the sauce and serve topped with the grilled cherry tomatoes.

Accompany with grated cheese.

Grains: Bulgur, Rice and Couscous

Wheat, along with the olive tree and the grape vine, was part of the famous triad that the Greeks and Romans planted throughout the ancient world, and is eaten today in the forms of pasta, bulgur (cracked wheat) in the eastern Mediterranean and couscous in North Africa. But while bulgur is the staple food of the eastern Mediterranean countryside, in the cities it is rice, first introduced by the Arabs, that is the everyday fare.

Bulgur with Cheese and Aubergines | serves 4–6

This Syrian dish, which combines bulgur with the chewy, salty *halumi* cheese and aubergines, can be served as a main course.

> *350g aubergines, cut into 3cm cubes*
> *salt*
> *1½ large onions, sliced*
> *sunflower or light vegetable oil*
> *350g bulgur, preferably coarsely ground*
> *800ml boiling water or vegetable stock (you may use a*
> *   stock cube)*
> *pepper*
> *200–250g halumi cheese, cubed*

Sprinkle the aubergines generously with salt and leave in a colander for 1 hour to degorge their juices, then rinse and dry with paper towels.

Fry the onions in 2 tbsp of oil over medium heat until golden. Add the bulgur and boiling water or vegetable stock. Season with salt and pepper and stir well, then cook over very low heat, covered, for about 15 minutes or until the water has been absorbed and the bulgur is tender.

Fry the cubed aubergines briefly in hot oil, turning them so that they are tender and lightly coloured all over. Lift out and drain on paper towels.

Stir 5 tbsp of oil into the bulgur. Add the cheese and the aubergines and gently mix them in. Heat through, covered, until the cheese is soft.

Serve immediately.

Bulgur Pilaf with Tomatoes | serves 4

Bulgur can be found coarsely ground in speciality stores. This dish can be served as an accompaniment to fish or mixed vegetable dishes, gratins or flans, egg dishes and cheese bakes.

1 medium onion, chopped
5 tbsp sunflower or vegetable oil
250g bulgur, preferably coarsely ground
4 medium tomatoes, peeled and chopped
500ml vegetable stock
salt and pepper
2 tbsp chopped fresh mint

Fry the onion in 2 tbsp of the oil over medium heat until soft. Add the bulgur, tomatoes and stock, salt, pepper and mint. Stir well and cook, covered, for 15 minutes or until the liquid is absorbed and holes appear at the top. Add the remaining oil, then turn off the heat and leave to sit, covered, for 20 minutes. Serve hot.

Bulgur Pilaf with Raisins and Pine Nuts | serves 4

This is another side dish that can be served with vegetarian flans and gratins, egg and cheese dishes, and mixed vegetables. It also goes well with fish dishes.

> *500ml vegetable stock*
> *5 tbsp sunflower or vegetable oil*
> *250g bulgur, preferably coarsely ground*
> *2 tbsp raisins*
> *salt and pepper*
> *3 tbsp pine nuts*

Bring the stock with 4 tbsp of oil to the boil. Add the bulgur and the raisins and a little salt and pepper (you may not need any salt as the stock is already salty).

Stir well and cook, covered, for 15 minutes, until the liquid is absorbed and holes appear at the top. Turn off the heat and leave to sit, covered, for 20 minutes.

Fry the pine nuts in the rest of the oil over medium heat, shaking the pan, until they are lightly golden. Stir them into the bulgur and serve.

Tomato Risotto | serves 4

There is a version of rice cooked with tomatoes in almost every country around the Mediterranean. This Provençal method uses wine to give a delicious flavour. It is a good accompaniment to vegetable flans and gratins, egg dishes, cheese bakes and mixed vegetables. It also makes a hearty first course.

> *1 garlic clove, finely chopped*
> *2 tbsp extra virgin olive oil*
> *500g (about 6 medium) tomatoes, peeled and chopped*
> *about 175ml dry white wine*
> *salt and pepper*
> *1–2 tsp granulated sugar, to taste*
> *250g arborio rice*

In a large pan, fry the garlic in the oil over low heat until it begins to colour.

Add the tomatoes, wine, salt, pepper and sugar and simmer for 15 minutes.

Add the rice and cook, covered, over very low heat, for about 20 minutes. Add a little more wine if it becomes too dry.

Serve hot or cold.

Rice with Spinach | serves 4

This beautiful Turkish pilaf is often accompanied by yoghurt. It can be served, like the other rice side dishes, to accompany most vegetable dishes and can also be a first course.

> *500g fresh spinach*
> *1 large onion, chopped*
> *4 tbsp light vegetable oil*
> *300g American long-grain rice*
> *500ml vegetable stock or water*
> *salt and pepper*
> *1 tsp granulated sugar*
> *juice of ½ lemon, or to taste*

Wash and drain the spinach and cut it coarsely or leave whole. Remove the stems only if they are tough.

Fry the onion in the oil in a large pan over medium heat until soft.

Add the rice and stir well, then add the stock or water, salt, pepper, sugar, lemon juice and the spinach. Stir well and cook, covered, over very low heat for about 18 minutes or until the rice is tender.

Serve hot or cold.

Note

Frozen leaf spinach, defrosted and coarsely chopped, may be used.

Variation

Serve 280ml plain yoghurt as an accompaniment, flavoured, if desired, with one crushed garlic clove.

Rice Pilaf with Raisins and Pine Nuts | serves 4

This is the standard pilaf found in Middle Eastern restaurants and cafeterias. It makes a good side dish for many of the vegetable dishes and can also be served cold.

> *1 large onion, chopped*
> *100ml sunflower oil*
> *4 tbsp pine nuts*
> *250g American long-grain rice*
> *salt*
> *½ tsp cinnamon*
> *¼ tsp allspice*
> *¼ tsp ground cardamom*
> *450ml boiling vegetable stock or water*
> *2–3 tbsp currants or raisins*

Fry the onion in about half the oil over medium heat until soft. Add the pine nuts and stir to brown them lightly all over.

Add the rice and stir to coat the grains with oil. Add the salt, cinnamon, allspice and cardamom.

Cover with the boiling stock or water, stir in the currants or raisins and mix well. Cook, covered, for 18–20 minutes, until the rice is tender.

Stir in the remaining oil and serve hot or cold.

Variation

At the end mix in a small tin of chick peas, drained, boiled in water and then drained again.

Risotto with Peas and Asparagus | serves 4–6

This Italian springtime risotto is light and fresh. I prefer it without the cream and cheese but some of my family prefer the richer version. Serve it as a first course or as a main dish.

> 1 large onion, chopped
> 50g butter
> 1 tbsp vegetable oil
> 300g arborio rice
> 500ml dry white wine
> salt and pepper
> 500ml vegetable stock made with 1 stock cube
> 250g podded baby peas
> 250g asparagus tips
> 150ml double cream (optional)
> 4 tbsp grated Parmesan cheese (optional)

In a large frying pan or sauté pan, fry the onion in half the amount of butter and all of the oil, over very low heat, until soft, stirring occasionally.

Add the rice, and stir until all the grains are coated with fat and become translucent. Pour in the white wine, season with salt and pepper and simmer gently until the wine is absorbed.

Gradually stir in the stock, a little at a time, adding more as it becomes absorbed, and water if necessary, until the rice is creamy but still al dente.

Meanwhile, cook the peas and asparagus in boiling salted water until they are just tender.

Stir the remaining butter, and the cream and cheese, if using, into the rice, and serve at once, topped with the drained vegetables.

Variation

Other vegetables could be added, such as sliced fennel or celery, sliced courgettes and broad beans.

Couscous

Couscous is the indigenous Berber food of North Africa. The word refers to the hard semolina grain on which it is based as well as to the stew or soup and the side dishes that go with it. In North Africa, it is served at the end of a festive meal, before the sweet, or as a one-dish family meal. Stews and soups are nearly always based on meat or chicken, or sometimes fish (see Fish Couscous with Quince on page 210–11).

A stew with vegetables only is considered a dish *de régime* for people on a diet. But with a good assortment of vegetables, it can be a truly glorious affair – a joy to look at and a pleasure to eat.

The combination of many different herbs and 'sweet' spices is part of the appeal.

Basic Method for Making Couscous

The couscous we get in Britain is a processed (pre-cooked) product. All you do is add salted water and oil and heat it through. When I visited a couscous factory in Sfax, Tunisia, the owner explained that their couscous could be heated in a saucepan, in the oven or the microwave.

I shamelessly make it the easiest way, as described in the packet instructions, with very good results. It is so easy you can make it for very large parties. Simply measure the volume of the grain and add the same volume of warm water – even a little less, as you can add more later if necessary.

For 6 to 8 people put 500g medium-ground couscous in a bowl. Add 600ml warm water with ½–1 tsp salt, stirring slowly so that the water is absorbed evenly.

After about 10–15 minutes, when the couscous has become a little plump and tender, add 3–4 tbsp groundnut or light vegetable oil and rub the grain between your hands to air it and break up any lumps. Heat it through by steaming in the top part of a *couscoussier* (it is ready as soon as the steam passes through the grain) or, more simply, in the oven, covered with foil, at 200°C/400°F/Gas6 for about 20 minutes.

When I make couscous for a large number of people, I put it straight into the huge clay dish I plan to serve it in, which goes into the oven. There is nothing easier.

A smaller quantity for 2 or 3 people can be heated in a saucepan, stirring to prevent it from burning. Before serving, break up any lumps very thoroughly.

Couscous with Roasted Vegetables serves 6

This is not a traditional North African dish but it is most appealing.

> *1 recipe Grilled or Roasted Vegetables (see page 125)*
>
> **For the bed of couscous**
> *500g couscous*
> *900ml water*
> *1½ vegetable stock cubes*
> *a little salt*
> *1-2 garlic cloves, crushed*
> *½–1 tsp cinnamon*
> *¼ tsp allspice*
> *¼ tsp powdered ginger*
> *¼ tsp saffron (optional)*
> *a good pinch of chilli powder*
> *4 tbsp chopped coriander*
> *2 tbsp chopped flat-leafed parsley*
> *4 tbsp sunflower or vegetable oil*
> *2 tbsp raisins, soaked in water for 10 minutes.*

Pre-heat the oven to 200°C/400°F/Gas 6.

Put the couscous in a large ovenproof serving dish.

Bring the water to the boil in a large pan. Add the stock cubes, salt (take into consideration the saltiness of the stock

Invitation to Mediterranean Cooking

cubes), garlic, cinnamon, allspice, ginger, saffron, if using, and chilli powder. Simmer for 8 minutes until the garlic is soft. Remove from the heat and add the coriander and parsley.

Pour 600ml of this hot 'soup' over the couscous (keep the rest to moisten the grain when you are serving) and stir well so that it is absorbed evenly. Leave for 15 minutes or until the grain is tender. Stir in the oil and rub the grain between your palms to fluff it up and separate and break up any lumps, then drain the raisins and add them to the couscous.

About 20 minutes before serving, heat the grain through, covered with foil, in the oven.

Reheat the soup and the Grilled or Roasted Vegetables. Break up any lumps in the couscous and serve, with the remaining soup poured over and the hot vegetables on top.

Vegetable Couscous | serves 10–12

The following recipe is for 10 or more because it is as easy to make for many as it is for a few and it is a good party dish. It can also be made in advance. It might seem daunting because of the number of ingredients but it is simply a matter of throwing vegetables into a pot. I give a long list of vegetables to choose from. Seven is a usual number, but you can have as many as you like and you can vary the quantities.

For the garnish
250g chick peas, soaked for at least 1 hour
salt
150g raisins

For the grain
1kg couscous
1.25 litres water
1–2 tsp salt
6 tbsp groundnut or vegetable oil

Vegetables to choose from for the stew or soup
2 large onions, sliced
500g (about 4 large) turnips, cut in half or left whole if
    baby ones
500g (about 4 large) carrots, peeled and cut in half
    lengthways

500g (4 medium) potatoes, peeled and quartered
1 small white cabbage, cut into 8 pieces through the heart
3 red peppers, cut into ribbons
5 artichoke hearts, cut in half (you may use frozen ones)
3 small fennel bulbs, quartered
500g broad beans or petits pois (you may use frozen ones)
4 medium tomatoes, peeled and quartered
500g piece of orange pumpkin, cut into 5cm pieces
500g (about 3–4) courgettes, cut into 5cm slices or in
    half lengthways

Aromatics
salt and pepper
2 tsp cinnamon
½ tsp allspice
1 tsp ground ginger
½ tsp saffron powder
¼ tsp chilli powder
a large bunch flat-leafed parsley, chopped
a large bunch coriander, chopped
a bunch rocket, coarsely chopped
a bunch cress, coarsely chopped

For the peppery sauce
2 tsp Harissa (see page 268) or more, to taste, or 2 tsp
    paprika and ¼–½ tsp or more chilli powder

Pre-heat the oven to 200°C/400°F/Gas 6.

To make the garnish, boil the chick peas in water for an hour or until tender, adding salt when they begin to soften. Boil the raisins separately for 15 minutes in enough water to cover.

Prepare the couscous grain as described on pages 111–12 in an ovenproof serving dish. About 20–30 minutes before serving, cover with foil and heat through in the oven (it will steam).

To prepare the stew or soup, put 2.5 litres water with 7 (or more) vegetables of your choice in a large saucepan. Bring to the boil and remove any scum. Add salt and pepper and the spices (but not the herbs) and simmer for 30 minutes or until all the vegetables are tender. Add the herbs and cook 5 more minutes.

To make the peppery sauce, put 2 ladlesful of liquid from the soup in a small bowl and stir in the Harissa or paprika and chilli powder.

Before serving, break up any lumps in the couscous very thoroughly, stir in a little of the broth, and shape the grain into a little mountain. Serve the vegetables in a separate bowl or arrange them on top of the couscous. Reheat the chick peas and raisins, and put them into separate bowls. Put them on the table along with the peppery sauce, and let people help themselves.

Mixed Vegetable Dishes

The wide range of Mediterranean vegetables and the magnificent flavour they acquire under the warm sun are legendary. The art of cooking them the Mediterranean way – a rich amalgam of food traditions inherited from the ancient world, from the Byzantine and Ottoman Empires, the Arabs, France, Italy and Spain – has been carried to all the corners of the world. Many of the dishes in this section are ideal party food. They can be served as side dishes and they also make spectacular main dishes, served simply with bread and cheese.

Vegetables Cooked in White Wine and Olive Oil

This Provençal method of cooking vegetables, in a mixture of white wine (I use a fruity dry Riesling) and olive oil, gives them a splendid flavour, and to some, a soft muted gold colour.

They retain a certain firmness of texture even when they are long-cooked. A beautiful assortment makes a grand party dish to serve hot or cold. You must cook the vegetables in batches, giving each the time they require, which is longer than is needed in boiling water. Asparagus and spring onions, for instance, take about 10 minutes; carrots and potatoes 45–60 minutes. Let them bubble gently over low heat with the lid on.

> *For the cooking liquor*
> *1 bottle (750ml) dry white wine*
> *175ml very light, mild-tasting or bland extra virgin*
>   *olive oil*
> *salt to taste*
> *2 sprigs of thyme*
> *4 bay leaves*

Put the wine and oil in a large pan with some salt, and the thyme and bay leaves. Bring to the boil (oil will combine with the wine as the mixture bubbles) then simmer over low heat. Cook the vegetables in batches, lifting them out and arranging them on a serving platter as they become tender. If you want

to serve them hot, heat through in the oven, covered with foil.
I particularly like them cold.

Suggestions

You can use asparagus, spring onions, shiitake mushrooms,
green beans, mange-tout, tiny onions, carrots, potatoes,
parsnips and turnips. To my surprise, my favourites for this
treatment are carrots, potatoes and parsnips. Most vegetables
are best left whole. Large carrots can be cut into thick slices or
in half lengthwise, and turnips, parsnips and potatoes cut into
slices or cubed.

Baby Vegetables Cooked in Stock |

About 10 years ago the chefs of Provence brought into fashion tiny baby vegetables and have since refined their ways of cooking them. If the variety of vegetables is large enough, you can serve the dish as the main part of a meal for four, or pile them on to a platter as the centrepiece for a dinner party. Perfectionists boil the vegetables separately as they cook at slightly different rates, even though they are all tiny.

> *2kg baby vegetables or new spring vegetables such as tiny*
> *   new potatoes, spring onions, asparagus spears, baby*
> *   courgettes, tiny leeks, small fennel bulbs and celery*
> *   hearts, pickling onions, green beans, mange-tout, baby*
> *   lettuces and sweetcorn*
> *about 2 litres vegetable stock – you may use stock cubes*
> *salt*
> *2–3 garlic cloves, chopped*
> *4 bay leaves*
> *2 sprigs of thyme*
>
> **For the dressing**
> *100ml very light, mild-tasting or bland extra virgin olive*
> *   oil or a mixture of olive and sunflower oil*
> *3 tbsp mixed chopped herbs, such as chervil, chives and*
> *   parsley*

Leave the vegetables whole. Wash them, peel them (or not, as desired), but leave the little stalks and leaves if they have them. Trim the roots and dark green ends of leeks and spring onions. Boil the vegetables in enough stock to cover, with salt if necessary, the garlic cloves, bay leaves and thyme, until al dente. Drain.

Make a dressing by mixing together the oil and herbs and pour over the vegetables.

Variation

To intensify the flavour you might like to add the juice of ½ lemon and 1tbsp granulated sugar to the stock.

Grilled or Roasted Vegetables | serves 4

Vegetables cooked on a barbecue or under the grill (broiler), or roasted at high heat in the oven, develop a rich intense flavour. All kinds of vegetables may be grilled, but those listed below are a typical Mediterranean combination. This recipe makes a wonderful meal in itself. The same roasted vegetables can be served over a couscous base (see page 115) or with pasta.

> *1 large aubergine, cut into 1–1.25cm slices lengthways*
> *salt*
> *4 medium courgettes, cut into 1–1.25cm slices lengthways*
> *2 medium mild onions, cut into thick slices*
> *2–4 plum tomatoes, cut in half*
> *2 red or yellow peppers, cut in half*
> *extra virgin olive oil*
> *4–8 fat garlic cloves in their skins*
> *pepper*
> *4 tbsp chopped herbs such as parsley, basil, chervil or*
>   *marjoram (optional)*

Sprinkle the aubergine slices with salt and leave them to degorge their bitter juices for 30 minutes, then rinse and dry them.

Brush the aubergine, courgettes, onions, tomatoes and peppers with oil.

Cook the aubergine, courgettes and onions on the barbecue

or under the grill until tender and browned, turning them over once. Do the peppers with the skin side only towards the heat. Be sure the aubergines are properly cooked – when underdone they are unpleasant (they are ready when they feel very soft when you prick them with a fork). Cook the tomatoes and garlic cloves until softened.

Alternatively, roast the sliced vegetables on trays lined with foil in a very hot (250°C/480°F/Gas10) oven, being careful that they do not overcook.

Arrange all the vegetables on a serving plate. The garlic cloves can be peeled or left in their skins.

Serve hot or cold, sprinkled with salt and pepper, a drizzle of olive oil and, if you like, chopped parsley and other fresh herbs.

Variations

If you serve the vegetables cold, you may like to squeeze a little lemon juice over them or sprinkle with a little sherry or balsamic vinegar.

For pasta with grilled or roasted vegetables, boil 400g pasta in salted water until al dente, then drain. Dress with 6 tbsp or more extra virgin olive oil mixed with 6 tbsp chopped flatleafed parsley and serve topped with the roasted vegetables.

Whole Roasted Vegetables | serves 4

This is another popular way of cooking vegetables in the Mediterranean – a plateful served with an assortment of good cheeses makes a perfect meal.

> *2 medium aubergines*
> *2 medium onions*
> *2 red peppers*
> *2 plum tomatoes*
> *1 whole head of garlic with fat cloves*
> *4–5 tbsp olive oil*
> *salt and pepper*

Pre-heat the oven to 180°C/350°F/Gas 4.

Prick the aubergines with a sharp knife to prevent them bursting. Put all the vegetables whole, as they are, on baking trays lined with foil. Roast them in the oven until soft. Take the tomatoes and garlic out after 20 minutes, when they soften. Leave the onions, peppers and aubergines in for about 1 hour until the skins are brown, turning them once.

Drop the peppers into a thick polythene bag and twist to seal it (this loosens the skin). When they are cool enough to handle, peel the vegetables and deseed the peppers. Cut the tomatoes in half, the onions in quarters, the peppers and aubergines into strips. Peel the garlic cloves and leave them whole.

Dress with the olive oil, salt and pepper and mix together. Serve cold.

Root Vegetables with Chestnuts | serves 4

It is worth making use of chestnuts in this engaging French way. You may use either frozen or vacuum-packed ones.

> 4 small turnips
> 1 large parsnip
> 1 large carrot
> 1 sweet potato (about 250g)
> 2 tbsp sunflower or vegetable oil
> stock made with 500ml water mixed with 1 vegetable
>   stock cube
> 100ml dry white wine (optional)
> salt and pepper
> 1 tbsp lemon juice
> 16 chestnuts

Peel the vegetables and cut them into 2.5cm cubes and put them in a pan.

Pour in the oil, stock and wine to cover. Season with salt and plenty of pepper, taking into consideration the saltiness of the stock, and add the lemon juice.

Simmer, uncovered, for about 25 minutes, or until the vegetables are just tender and the liquid is reduced to a sauce.

Meanwhile, prepare the chestnuts. To peel them, make a slit in their flat side with a pointed knife and roast them under the grill for 2 minutes, turning them over once, until they blacken slightly. Peel them as soon as they are cool enough to handle. Drop them into the pan with the vegetables and cook in the sauce for 5 minutes or longer. Raise the heat to high, if necessary, to reduce the sauce.

Serve hot.

Mixed Vegetable Fritters

Italians are famous for their deep-fried vegetables in batter – *fritti misti di verdura* – which vary in content from one region to another and to which, in the south, they sometimes add egg-and-breadcrumbed pieces of mozzarella, and in the north, lumps of fried, slightly sweet, thick 'cream' (actually milk cooked with ground rice) and pieces of fruit such as sliced apple. But every other country in the Mediterranean has some version of vegetable fritters too. Turks specialize in fried aubergine and courgette slices, which they serve with yoghurt or with a Fresh Tomato Sauce (see page 271).

For the batter
150g plain flour
½ tsp salt
1 tsp baking powder
1 tbsp extra virgin olive oil
1 large egg yolk
about 200ml water or soda water

For the vegetables
Choose a variety from the following: fat spring onions, trimmed of their roots and dark green ends; asparagus (trimmed of their tough ends); button mushrooms; courgettes, sliced lengthways; aubergines, sliced into rounds 1cm thick; cauliflower, boiled first then cut into florets; artichoke bottoms, cut into slices

sunflower or vegetable oil for deep frying
salt and pepper
1 lemon, cut into wedges

To make the batter, mix the flour, salt and baking powder in a large bowl, and add the oil and egg yolk. Vigorously beat in enough of the water to make a light creamy batter. Leave to rest for 30 minutes and beat again before using.

To make the fritters, dip the vegetables in the batter and deep-fry in sizzling, medium-hot oil until crisp and lightly browned and tender inside. Drain on paper towels.

Serve at once, sprinkled with salt and pepper, and accompanied with lemon wedges. Reheat, if necessary, in the oven.

Broad Beans, Turnips and Spinach | serves 4–6

It is best to use fresh vegetables but frozen broad beans and frozen whole leaf spinach will do very well.

> *500g (about 5) small turnips, peeled*
> *200g shelled broad beans*
> *1 garlic clove, finely chopped*
> *3 tbsp sunflower or vegetable oil*
> *juice of ½ lemon*
> *1–2 tsp granulated sugar*
> *1 tsp dried mint*
> *about 4 tbsp water*
> *250g spinach*
> *salt and pepper*

Cut the turnips in half then into 1cm slices. Put them in a large pan with the beans, garlic and oil, and sauté over very low heat for 5–10 minutes until lightly coloured.

Add the lemon juice, sugar, mint and water and cook for about 10–20 minutes, until the vegetables are tender.

Meanwhile, wash and drain the spinach (remove the stems only if they are tough), and press out the excess water. When the beans and turnips have almost finished cooking, add the spinach to the pan. Put the lid on so that the leaves cook in the steam for a minute or two, until they crumple. Stir well and adjust the seasoning.

Serve hot or cold.

Note

If using frozen beans and spinach, simply defrost and add to the pan when the turnips are tender, then cook for a few more minutes.

Omelettes
and Egg Dishes

The Mediterranean is famous for its egg dishes and omelettes. The latter are usually like thick cakes, filled with vegetables, and can be eaten hot or cold. Accompanied with salad they make a good family meal, and because they can be made in advance, they are an easy option for entertaining and buffet meals. They are colourful and can look quite elegant, cut into wedges or little squares and garnished with cress. They are also traditional picnic foods.

Spinach Omelette | serves 4

Every Arab country has a version of spinach omelette. This one is Egyptian.

> *250g spinach (you may use frozen leaf spinach)*
> *1 large onion, chopped*
> *4 tbsp sunflower or light vegetable oil*
> *1 large tomato, peeled and chopped*
> *salt and pepper*
> *4 large eggs*
> *¼ tsp nutmeg*

Wash and drain the fresh spinach and squeeze the water out between your hands. Remove the stems only if they are tough. Put it in a saucepan over a low heat and cover with the lid. The spinach will cook in the steam of the water that clings to it and crumple very quickly to a soft mass. Drain in a colander and press all the water out.

If using frozen spinach, thaw thoroughly and press all the water out.

Fry the onion in 2 tbsp of the oil until golden. Add the tomato, salt and pepper and cook for 15 minutes or until the sauce is reduced.

Beat the eggs lightly in a bowl with salt, pepper and the nutmeg. Add the tomato sauce and the spinach, and mix well.

Heat the rest of the oil in a frying pan (preferably a non-stick pan). Pour in the spinach and egg mixture and cook over a low heat for about 10 minutes until the bottom of the omelette sets firm. Put the pan under the grill and cook until the top of the omelette is firm and lightly browned.

Serve hot or cold, cut into wedges.

Aubergine Omelette | serves 4

Maacoudes – omelettes that combine all kinds of ingredients – are among the most popular hors-d'oeuvres in Tunisia. They are served hot or cold. This one has a lovely, subtle texture and flavour.

> 750g (about 2 medium) aubergines
> 1 large onion, chopped
> 4 tbsp olive oil
> 3 garlic cloves, crushed
> 4 large eggs
> 3 tbsp flat-leafed parsley, coarsely chopped
> ½–1 tsp ground caraway seeds
> ½ tsp ground coriander
> salt and pepper
> 1 lemon, cut into wedges

Prick the aubergines in a few places with a pointed knife to prevent them from bursting. Put them on a baking tray under the grill for about 20 minutes, turning them until their skin is black and the flesh feels soft when you press them.

Fry the onion in 2 tbsp of the oil over a very low heat until golden, stirring occasionally. Add the garlic and stir until lightly coloured.

Put the aubergines in a colander and peel them. Chop the flesh with two knives in the colander, then mash it with a fork, allowing the juices to run out.

In a bowl, beat the eggs lightly. Add the mashed aubergine, the onion, garlic, parsley, caraway, coriander, salt and pepper. Mix well.

Heat the remaining oil in a large, preferably non-stick, frying pan. Pour in the mixture and cook, covered, over a very low heat for about 10 minutes until the bottom has set. Put the frying pan under the grill and cook until the top is firm and lightly browned.

Serve hot or cold accompanied with the lemon wedges.

Five Vegetable Omelette | serves 4

In the south of France this dish is called a *tian bohémienne*. In North Africa a mixture of fried vegetables with eggs in a frying pan is a *shakshouka*. All kinds of vegetables can go into a *shak - shouka*, including peas, broad beans and pumpkin, but the most popular combination is that usually found in ratatouille. The French deep-fry the vegetables separately then drain them, mix them with the rest of the ingredients and bake them, but sautéing them all in the frying pan is quicker and equally good.

> *1 onion, coarsely chopped*
> *6 tbsp extra virgin olive oil, or as required*
> *2 garlic cloves, chopped*
> *1 medium aubergine cut into 1.5cm cubes*
> *2 medium courgettes, cut into 1.25cm slices*
> *1 red pepper, cut into 1.5cm strips*
> *4 medium tomatoes, peeled and chopped*
> *salt and pepper*
> *1 tsp granulated sugar*
> *1 sprig of thyme, crumbled*
> *4 tbsp chopped parsley*
> *4 large eggs, lightly beaten*

In a large frying pan, fry the onion in 2 tbsp of the oil until soft.

Add the garlic, aubergine, courgettes, pepper and the rest of the oil and sauté, over high then medium heat, turning the vegetables over frequently, until lightly coloured.

Add the tomatoes, salt, pepper, sugar and thyme, and cook until the vegetables are tender.

Add the parsley and eggs, a little more salt and pepper, stir very gently, and cook until the eggs have set.

Serve hot with bread.

Variation

Break the eggs over the vegetables and cook them whole.

Spanish Potato Tortilla | serves 4–5

The tortilla is the most popular appetizer served in Spanish bars, but it can also be the centre of a family meal. It can be made in advance and reheated or eaten cold.

> *2 large potatoes, peeled and cut into 0.5cm slices*
> *1 large Spanish onion, thinly sliced*
> *salt*
> *125ml oil – a mixture of olive oil and light vegetable oil*
> *3 large eggs, lightly beaten*

Sprinkle the potatoes and onion lightly with salt.

Heat the oil in a non-stick frying pan and add the potatoes and onions at the same time. Cook slowly over a medium heat (it is really stewing rather than frying), for about 15 minutes, stirring occasionally, until the vegetables are tender but not brown.

Drain the vegetables in a colander, reserving the oil.

In a bowl, mix the potatoes and onion with the eggs and leave to soak for about 15 minutes.

Wipe the frying pan clean and heat 2 tbsp of the reserved oil to sizzling hot. Pour in the potato and egg mixture and lower the heat to medium-low. Shake the pan occasionally to prevent the tortilla from sticking. When it starts to come away from the sides of the pan and the bottom has browned a little, turn over the tortilla by placing a large plate over the frying pan and quickly turning the tortilla upside-down on to it. Add another tablespoon of the oil to the frying pan and quickly slide the tortilla back in. Cook the other side for a minute. Alternatively, brown under the grill.

Serve hot or cold, cut into wedges.

Egg and Tomato | serves 2

When one of my children arrives unexpectedly at meal time, Egg and Tomato is one of the things I rustle up. It is a common standby in Egypt. Often, I do not bother to peel the tomatoes, and it makes no difference to the end result.

> *3 garlic cloves, or to taste, chopped*
> *3 tbsp sunflower or extra virgin olive oil*
> *4 plum tomatoes, cut into 1cm slices*
> *salt and pepper*
> *⅔ tsp granulated sugar*
> *4 large eggs*
> *3 tbsp chopped basil, coriander or parsley*

In a large frying pan, fry the garlic in the oil until it begins to colour.

Add the tomatoes, preferably in one layer, and season lightly with salt, pepper and sugar. Cook for 2–3 minutes then turn over the tomato slices.

Break open the eggs on top of the tomatoes and sprinkle with salt and pepper. Cook over gentle heat until the eggs have set.

Serve hot, sprinkled with the chopped herbs. Accompany with bread.

Variations

Peel and chop the tomatoes. Cook as described and when they have softened, add the eggs and scramble them gently. Serve them soft and creamy.

Add a few black olives, pitted and cut into pieces.

Eggs Baked with Peppers and Tomatoes

serves 4

This delectable Tunisian dish is called a *tagine* after the shallow clay dish in which it is cooked.

> 2 red peppers
> 1 medium onion, chopped
> 2 tbsp olive or sunflower oil
> 500g (about 6 medium) tomatoes, peeled and diced
> salt and pepper
> 1–2 tsp granulated sugar
> 2 tbsp capers (optional)
> ½–1 tsp Harissa (see page 268) or 1 tsp paprika and a
>   good pinch of cayenne or red chilli powder (optional)
> 4 large eggs, lightly beaten

Pre-heat the oven to 180°C/350°F/Gas 4.

Grill the peppers (for directions see page 263), peel and cut the flesh into ribbons.

Fry the onion in the oil until golden. Add the tomatoes, salt, pepper and sugar and simmer for about 20 minutes until the sauce is reduced.

Remove from the heat and add the capers, the Harissa, diluted in a tablespoon of water, or the paprika and cayenne.

Let the mixture cool a little, then beat in the eggs.

Put the peppers in an oiled baking dish (about 23cm

diameter) and pour the egg mixture on top. Bake for 50 minutes or until set. Serve hot.

Variations

To make it a substantial dish, add 2 boiled, peeled and diced potatoes or a drained 400g tin of white haricot beans.

You may also add a handful of grated Gruyère or crumbled feta.

Flans, Gratins and Cheese Bakes

These baked vegetable dishes with eggs and cheese make ideal vegetarian meals because they contain all the necessary proteins, carbohydrates, fibre and nutrients. They are also extremely satisfying and have an added advantage in that they can be made in advance and reheated before serving. French *tians* and Italian *pasticcio* are creamy, with a béchamel base, while the Arab equivalents are often made with eggs. Serve them as main dishes, accompanied with salad. They are delicious both hot and cold and are perfect for buffet meals.

Courgette Cake with Tomato Sauce | serves 4

The olives and capers in the sauce lift the delicate flavours of the courgettes and creamy custard of this Provençal flan.

>*1 large onion, chopped*
>*1½ tbsp olive oil*
>*4 large eggs*
>*125ml milk*
>*salt and white pepper*
>*a pinch of nutmeg*
>*500g (about 4 largish) courgettes, very thinly sliced*
>
>*For the sauce*
>*1–2 garlic cloves, finely chopped*
>*1 tbsp olive oil*
>*500g (about 6 medium) tomatoes, peeled and chopped*
>*salt and pepper*
>*1–2 tsp granulated sugar*
>*1–2 tbsp coarsely chopped black olives*
>*1–2 tbsp capers, squeezed to remove excess vinegar*

Pre-heat the oven to 180°C/305°F/Gas 4.

Fry the onion in the oil over medium heat until very soft and golden, stirring often. Set aside.

Beat the eggs lightly with a fork, then beat in the milk and add salt, pepper and nutmeg. Add the fried onion and the courgettes and mix well.

Pour into a 26cm well-greased flan mould or baking dish. Bake for 1½ hours or until firm (cover with foil for the first hour so that the top does not over-brown).

Meanwhile, prepare the sauce. Fry the garlic in the oil over low heat, stirring, until slightly coloured. Add the tomatoes, salt, pepper and sugar and simmer for 20 minutes until reduced. Add the olives and capers and cook for a few more minutes.

Serve the courgette cake with the sauce poured over.

Courgette Gratin | serves 4

This is a dish from the Arab Mediterranean where it is often served with yoghurt. I have substituted Cheddar for the usual feta cheese because it complements the courgettes particularly well.

> *1 large onion, coarsely chopped*
> *2 tbsp sunflower or vegetable oil*
> *750g courgettes, cut into 1cm slices*
> *salt*
> *3 large eggs, lightly beaten*
> *200g grated (medium) Cheddar cheese*
> *white pepper*
> *a few gratings of nutmeg*

Pre-heat the oven to 180°C/350°F/Gas 4.

Fry the onion in the oil over medium heat until golden. Next, poach the courgettes in salted water for a few minutes only (they should be slightly underdone) and drain.

Mix the eggs with the fried onion and cheese, add the pepper and nutmeg, and fold in the courgettes.

Pour into a greased baking dish and bake for about 30 minutes or until set and lightly browned.

Aubergine, Tomato and Fontina Cheese Flan

serves 6

This *pasticcio di melanzane* hails from southern Italy.

> 750g aubergines, cut into 1cm slices
> salt
> 1 large onion, chopped
> sunflower oil for frying
> 750g tomatoes, peeled and chopped
> pepper
> 2 tsp granulated sugar
> 200g Fontina cheese, thinly sliced
> 500ml milk
> 4 large eggs
> 2 tbsp grated Parmesan cheese

Soak the aubergines for 30 minutes in water with plenty of salt. Rinse, drain and dry them.

To make a tomato sauce, fry the onion in 2 tbsp of oil until golden. Add the tomatoes, salt, pepper and sugar and cook for 15–20 minutes.

Pre-heat the oven to 180°C/350°F/Gas 4.

Deep-fry the aubergine slices in hot oil very briefly, turning them over once, until slightly browned, then drain on paper towels. Alternatively, you can grill the slices – brush them generously with oil, arrange them on an oven tray and cook them under a hot grill, turning to brown them on both sides.

In a baking dish, put layers of aubergine, Fontina cheese and tomato sauce.

Beat the milk with the eggs and Parmesan, add salt and pepper and pour over the dish.

Bake for 1¼ hours or until set. Serve hot.

Baked Aubergines with Tomato Sauce and Feta Cheese | serves 4

This is the Arab equivalent of the famous Italian *parmigiana di melanzane*.

> 1 recipe Fresh Tomato Sauce (see page 271)
> 500g (1 large or 2 medium) aubergines, cut into round
>   1cm slices
> salt
> vegetable or sunflower oil for frying
> pepper
> 4 tbsp chopped flat-leafed parsley
> 100g feta cheese, mashed with a fork
> 3 large eggs

Pre-heat the oven to 200°C/400°F/Gas 6.

Make the Fresh Tomato Sauce as directed on page 271.

Sprinkle the aubergine with salt and leave for 30 minutes until the juices are drawn out. Then rinse off the salt and dry with paper towels. Fry the slices very briefly in very hot oil (so that they absorb as little oil as possible), turning them over once, until browned. Drain on paper towels and arrange on the bottom of a 28cm baking dish.

Sprinkle with pepper and parsley and spoon a layer of the tomato sauce over them.

Beat the feta cheese with the eggs until well blended and spoon this mixture over the tomato sauce.

Bake for 20–30 minutes until set. Serve hot.

Variations

For a *parmigiana di melanzane*, use a small bunch of torn basil leaves instead of the parsley. Instead of feta, top with 250g diced mozzarella cheese and 6 tbsp grated Parmesan (with no eggs).

A French version uses béchamel sauce mixed with grated Gruyère as the topping.

Baked Pumpkin Cream | serves 4

This creamy *tian de courge* of the Vaucluse in the south of France has a sweet, delicate flavour that everyone loves. It can be served as a first course or as a main dish if accompanied by a Fresh Tomato Sauce (see page 271).

You need the orange-fleshed pumpkin that you find in Indian, Greek and Middle Eastern stores almost throughout the year. They are very large and are sold by the slice with seeds and fibres removed.

> *750g orange pumpkin (weight with skin but without*
>   *seeds and fibres)*
> *salt and white pepper*
> *a pinch of nutmeg*
> *1 small onion, chopped*
> *15g butter*
> *1 tbsp vegetable oil*
> *1 tbsp plain flour*
> *250ml milk*
> *2 large eggs, lightly beaten*
> *2–3 tbsp grated Gruyère cheese*

Pre-heat the oven to 200°C/400°F/Gas 6.

Peel the pumpkin and cut it into pieces. Put the pieces in a pan with about 4 tbsp water. Put the lid on and steam for about 15 minutes until very soft. Mash with a potato masher or fork, and add salt, pepper and nutmeg. Cook, stirring, over medium heat for a few minutes, until most of the liquid has evaporated (pumpkin releases a lot of water).

Fry the onion in the butter and oil over medium heat until soft but not brown. Add the flour and cook, stirring, for a minute or so.

Gradually add the milk, a little at a time, stirring to prevent lumps from forming, and cook over low heat until the white sauce thickens.

Mix the sauce with the pumpkin and the eggs, and beat well. Pour into a well-buttered 23cm baking dish. Sprinkle with grated Gruyère and bake for 40 minutes or until the top is slightly firm and golden.

Pumpkin Gratin | serves 4

This recipe is from the Eastern Mediterranean.

> *750g orange pumpkin (weight with skin but without*
> *seeds and fibres)*
> *about 5 tbsp water*
> *2 large eggs, lightly beaten*
> *100g feta cheese, mashed*
> *4 tbsp grated Parmesan cheese*

Pre-heat the oven to 180°C/350°F/Gas 4.

Peel the pumpkin and cut it into pieces. Put the pieces in a pan with the water and steam, with the lid on, for 15 minutes or until very soft. (Pumpkin will release quite a lot of liquid.) Mash it with a fork and cook over medium heat, stirring, for a few minutes until most of the liquid has evaporated.

Beat the eggs with the feta and Parmesan, then mix with the pumpkin. The cheeses are salty and you should not need to add extra salt, but taste to find out.

Pour into a greased 20cm baking dish and bake for about 25 minutes or until firm.

Baked Spinach with Eggs and Cheese | serves 4

This *tian d'épinards*, a speciality of the Vaucluse, is a homely, satisfying dish.

> 400g fresh or frozen spinach
> ½ onion, chopped
> 25g butter
> 2 tbsp plain flour
> 300ml boiling milk
> salt and pepper
> a pinch of nutmeg
> 2 large eggs, lightly beaten
> 2 large hard-boiled eggs, cut into pieces
> 50g grated Gruyère

Pre-heat the oven to 200°C/400°F/Gas 6.

If using fresh spinach, wash and drain it (remove the stems only if they are hard). Cook the leaves in a covered pan with no added water (they steam in the water that clings to them) until they crumple. Drain in a colander, reserving the juice. If using frozen whole leaf spinach, defrost and press out the excess water.

In a pan, fry the onion in the butter over low heat until soft. Add the flour and stir. Gradually stir in the milk and the spinach juice and cook for 5 minutes, stirring constantly to prevent lumps from forming.

Add salt, pepper and nutmeg, the lightly beaten eggs and the spinach, and beat well.

Fold in the hard-boiled eggs and the Gruyère and pour into a greased 23cm baking dish. Bake for 40 minutes or until slightly firm and golden on top.

Variation

Use a mixture of sorrel or other green leaves such as lettuce with the spinach, and add a few pitted black olives.

Vegetable Side Dishes

Anyone who has walked through a Mediterranean vegetable market knows how enthralling an experience it can be, with so much colourful fresh produce to choose from. Side dishes in Mediterranean countries are not the tasteless boiled or steamed vegetables we are used to here. They can be beguiling, yet simple at the same time. Serve them with egg dishes, flans and gratins, or with fish.

Herby New Potatoes | serves 4

In this traditional Provençal method of cooking potatoes, they are boiled with garlic and herbs and absorb the flavours through their skins. I like to use the tiny new potatoes now available in our supermarkets. Bring them to the table with the halved garlic heads, which are good to eat, and the sprigs of herbs.

> *750g baby new potatoes*
> *2 whole heads of garlic, cut in half crosswise*
> *3 bay leaves*
> *3 sprigs of thyme*
> *1 fresh chilli pepper*
> *salt and pepper*
> *extra virgin olive oil*

Rinse and scrub the potatoes. Put them in a pan with enough water to cover and add the rest of the ingredients, except the pepper and the oil.

Simmer until the potatoes are tender. Leave them in the cooking water to absorb the flavours until you are ready to serve.

Drain and serve, hot or cold, with a drizzle of olive oil and a sprinkling of salt and pepper.

Mashed Potatoes with Olive Oil and Parsley

serves 4

This dish can be eaten hot or cold and goes well with fish.

> *750g (about 4 large) floury potatoes*
> *6 tbsp extra virgin olive oil*
> *salt and pepper*
> *4 tbsp chopped flat-leafed parsley*

Peel the potatoes and boil them in salted water until soft. Drain, reserving about 100ml of the cooking water.

Mash the potatoes. Beat in the olive oil, add salt and pepper to taste and enough of the cooking water to achieve a soft, slightly moist texture. Stir in the parsley and serve hot.

Variation

Add 3 tbsp capers or chopped pitted black olives and fold them in.

Potatoes Stewed in Fresh Tomato Sauce

serves 4

I discovered this potato dish in Provence.

> *1 onion, chopped*
> *2 tbsp extra virgin olive oil*
> *2 garlic cloves, chopped*
> *400g tomatoes (about 5–6), peeled and chopped*
> *2 tsp granulated sugar*
> *salt and pepper*
> *2 sprigs of thyme, chopped*
> *750g new potatoes, cut into 2cm cubes*
> *about 200ml vegetable stock (you may use ½ stock cube*
> *   dissolved in ¾ cup water)*
> *2 tbsp chopped flat-leafed parsley*

Fry the onion in the oil until golden. Add the garlic and cook, stirring, until the aroma rises.

Add the tomatoes, sugar, salt, pepper and thyme, and simmer for about 15 minutes. Put in the potatoes, cover with the stock, and simmer gently until the potatoes are tender and the sauce has reduced. Stir in the parsley and serve.

Spinach Mousse | serves 4

This wonderfully creamy French mousse can be served with fish or as a first course with Fresh Tomato Sauce (see page 271) and a sprinkling of Parmesan. It is equally delicious served hot, with a hot sauce, or cold with a cold sauce.

> *375g fresh spinach*
> *150ml double cream*
> *1 large egg*
> *salt and pepper*

Pre-heat the oven to 180°C/350°F/Gas 4.

Wash the spinach and remove the stems only if they are tough. Drain and press out the excess water. Put the leaves in a pan and cook, covered, over low heat until they crumple into a soft mass. (They will steam in the water that clings to them.) Drain and squeeze out the juice, then blend the leaves to a paste in a food processor.

Add the cream and egg, and a little salt and pepper, and blend to a light homogenous cream.

Pour into a well-buttered, preferably non-stick, 20cm mould or cake tin and bake for 30 minutes or until the top seems slightly firm. Turn out while still hot – it should come out easily.

Variation

For a quicker and equally delicious dish, fry 1 crushed garlic clove in 1 tbsp sunflower oil, add the washed spinach leaves, and when they soften, add the double cream, salt, pepper and a pinch of nutmeg.

White Haricot Bean Pot | serves 6

This is a good hot or cold accompaniment to egg dishes, flans and gratins, and fish. The vegetables and herbs lend a delicious flavour.

> *500g small white haricot beans, soaked in water for*
>   *2 hours*
> *1 medium carrot, cut into 4 slices*
> *1 medium onion, quartered*
> *a few celery leaves*
> *2 garlic cloves, peeled*
> *2 medium tomatoes, peeled and chopped*
> *2 sprigs of rosemary*
> *1 bay leaf*
> *white pepper*
> *salt*
> *extra virgin olive oil*

Drain the beans and put them in a pot with the rest of the ingredients, except the salt and oil. Cover with water and simmer for 1 hour or until tender, adding salt towards the end.

Drain and serve hot or cold with a drizzle of olive oil.

Sautéed Courgettes | serves 4–6

Courgettes sautéed in oil have a much better taste than boiled ones. These can be served hot, or cold with lemon juice.

> *500g (about 3–4 largish) courgettes, cut into thin slices*
> *4 tbsp mild extra virgin olive oil or sunflower oil*
> *1 garlic clove, finely chopped*
> *salt and pepper*
> *2 tsp dried mint*
> *juice of ½ lemon (optional)*

In a large frying pan, sauté the courgettes in the oil over medium heat with the garlic, season with salt and pepper and turn the slices over a few times, until they are tender.

Add the mint towards the end, and the lemon juice, if using.

Sautéed Artichoke Hearts and Potatoes

serves 4

This is easy to make with frozen artichokes (available from Middle Eastern stores). It can be served as a first course.

> *1 garlic clove, crushed*
> *4–5 tbsp extra virgin olive oil*
> *8 frozen artichoke hearts or bottoms, defrosted and cut into slices*
> *4 medium-sized new potatoes, boiled, skinned and sliced*
> *salt and pepper*

Fry the garlic in the oil over low heat for a few seconds, stirring. Add the artichokes and sauté, stirring, until tender. Add the potatoes, season with salt and pepper, and cook, stirring, for a few minutes more until the potatoes are heated through. Serve hot.

Okra in Tomato Sauce | serves 4

Okra is a vegetable much loved in the eastern Mediterranean. But, unlike the aubergine, which the Turks claim to serve in a hundred different ways, *bamia* is almost always cooked with onions and tomatoes. It is served hot, with rice, or cold, as an appetizer.

> *400g okra, preferably young and small*
> *1 medium onion, cut in half and sliced*
> *3 tbsp vegetable or light extra virgin olive oil*
> *2 garlic cloves, chopped*
> *4 medium tomatoes, peeled and chopped*
> *salt and pepper*
> *juice of ½ lemon*
> *1–2 tsp granulated sugar, to taste*
> *a small bunch flat-leafed parsley or coriander, chopped*

Trim the conical caps and wash and drain the okra.

Fry the onion in the oil over medium heat until golden. Add the garlic and sauté for a moment or two.

Put in the okra and sauté for about 5 minutes, turning over the pods. Add the tomatoes, salt, pepper, lemon juice and sugar and cook for 15 minutes. Stir in the herbs before serving.

Sautéed Pumpkin with Raisins and Pine Nuts

serves 4

The raisin and pine nut partnership is something the Arabs brought to the Mediterranean region, all the way to Spain and Sicily. You find the garnish with spinach, rice, bulgur and all kinds of dishes. It goes well with pumpkin in this North African dish, which provides a certain delicate sweetness to a vegetarian meal.

1 large onion, sliced
3 tbsp groundnut or vegetable oil
500g pumpkin, cut into 2cm cubes
salt and plenty of pepper
1 tsp granulated sugar, or to taste (optional)
1 tsp cinnamon
3 tbsp raisins
3 tbsp pine nuts

In a large frying pan, fry the onion in the oil over medium heat, stirring occasionally, until soft and golden.

Add the pumpkin and sauté over low heat for 5 minutes, turning the pieces over.

Add salt, pepper, sugar, cinnamon and raisins. Cover with a tight-fitting lid and cook for about 20 minutes or until the pumpkin is tender, turning the pumpkin over occasionally. It will release its own juices.

Dry-toast the pine nuts or fry them in just a film of oil in a frying pan, shaking the pan to brown them lightly all over.

Serve the pumpkin hot or cold, sprinkled with the pine nuts.

Fish and Seafood

Much of Mediterranean fish cookery is a matter of grilling, frying, roasting or poaching, and marrying the fish with a dressing or sauce. Choose your fish and cook it by one of the methods on pages 191 to 206. Serve it with one of the marinades, dressings or sauces on pages 181 to 190. Popular Mediterranean fish include sea bass, sea bream, sole, gurnard, John Dory, red mullet, hake and tuna. Most of them are easy to obtain, but you can substitute fish from other seas, such as cod, haddock, halibut, snapper and catfish.

Oil and Lemon Dressing | serves 4

This is the standard, all-purpose Mediterranean dressing for fish.

juice of 1 lemon
6 tbsp extra virgin olive oil
salt and pepper
3 tbsp finely chopped flat-leafed parsley

Mix the ingredients cold and pour over the fish.

Warm Lemon and Tomato Dressing | serves 4

This is particularly delicious with grilled fish.

> *125ml light extra virgin olive oil*
> *juice of ½ lemon*
> *4 medium tomatoes, skinned and diced*
> *salt and pepper*
> *1–1½ tsp granulated sugar*

Simply put the oil, lemon juice, tomatoes, salt, pepper and sugar in a pan and heat through.

Sauce Vierge | serves 4

This spicy raw tomato sauce goes well with raw marinated fish and with cold fish.

> 3 medium tomatoes
> ¼–1 small red chilli
> 1 garlic clove, crushed
> 2.5cm piece of ginger, grated (or use the juice, pressed out using a garlic press)
> ½ red onion, finely chopped
> juice of ½ lime or lemon
> 4 tbsp extra virgin olive oil
> salt and pepper
> 1 tsp granulated sugar

Skin and finely chop the tomatoes, and finely chop the chilli. Mix with the rest of the ingredients to taste.

Chermoula | serves 4

This hot, spicy, garlicky mixture is the all-purpose, ubiquitous Moroccan sauce for fish. It goes on every kind of fish – fried, grilled, baked and stewed. Use half the quantity to marinate the fish for 30 minutes before cooking, and pour the rest on as a sauce before serving.

1 large bunch coriander, chopped
4 garlic cloves, crushed
1 tsp ground cumin
1 tsp paprika
¼–½ tsp chilli powder (optional)
6 tbsp groundnut or light extra virgin olive oil
juice of 1 lemon or 3 tbsp white wine vinegar

Blend all the ingredients together in a food processor.

Garlic Purée | serves 4–6

Cooks in Provence have many ways of turning garlic into something mild and delicate. This *purée d'ail*, in which garlic is simmered in white wine, is delicious with all kinds of fish. I have tried it with pan-fillet of whiting and also with grilled bream. Spread it on just before serving.

> *2 heads of garlic, preferably young, with fat cloves*
> *250ml dry white wine*
> *2 tbsp extra virgin olive oil*
> *salt and pepper*

Peel the garlic cloves and boil them in the wine for 15–20 minutes or until very soft. Drain and mash to a purée with a fork, then stir in the oil and a little salt and pepper.

Salsa Verde | serves 6

This Italian herb sauce is a good accompaniment to marinated and cold poached fish. The sauce keeps well in a jar with a layer of oil at the top.

> *a very large bunch flat-leafed parsley, stems removed*
> *75g pine nuts*
> *5 small gherkins*
> *8 pitted green olives*
> *3 garlic cloves, crushed*
> *3 tbsp white wine vinegar or the juice of ½ lemon*
> *salt and pepper*
> *about 250ml light extra virgin olive oil*

Blend all the ingredients except the oil in a food processor, then add the oil gradually – enough to achieve a light paste.

Tarator | serves 6

This lemony pine nut sauce is often seen on grand Arab buffet tables spread all over a large skinned, boned and re-shaped poached fish, but a dollop of it is equally good with a piece of cold fish.

> *1 slice of white bread, crusts removed*
> *175g pine nuts*
> *juice of 1–2 lemons, to taste*
> *1–2 garlic cloves, crushed*
> *salt and white pepper*
> *120ml sesame or vegetable oil*

Soak the bread in water and squeeze dry. Put it in a food processor with the pine nuts, lemon juice and garlic, a little salt and pepper, and purée, gradually adding enough oil to achieve a creamy mixture with the consistency of mayonnaise.

Romesco | serves 12

I love this roast pepper and almond sauce. It is an approximation of the famous Spanish sauce based on the dark, wine-coloured *ñora* peppers, which are sweet and slightly hot. The rich nutty, piquant flavour makes it a delightful accompaniment to vegetables as well as fish. It keeps well in a jar with a film of olive oil at the top. Serve it with grilled, steamed or fried fish and seafood, and with fish stews and soups.

> 2 red peppers
> 500g (about 6 medium) tomatoes
> 1 large slice of white bread, crusts removed
> 5 tbsp extra virgin olive oil
> 3 garlic cloves, crushed
> 100g blanched almonds
> juice of ½ lemon, or more to taste
> ½ red chilli pepper
> salt and pepper

Roast the peppers (see page 263) and tomatoes under the grill. Skin them and deseed the peppers.

Fry the bread in 2 tbsp of the oil over medium heat until golden, turning it over once. Add the garlic and stir until it just begins to colour.

Toast the almonds in a dry frying pan, shaking the pan to brown them all over.

In a food processor, blend the fried bread, garlic, almonds, the remaining oil, lemon juice and chilli to a paste. Add the peppers, tomatoes and salt and pepper, and blend to a creamy consistency.

Serve in a bowl and pass round for people to help themselves.

Variation

Blanched hazelnuts or a mixture of almonds and hazelnuts can be used instead.

Onion Fondue with Honey | serves 4

Use this to accompany or to stuff a fish. Because the fondue (the onions are melting soft, hence the name) is sweet, it is best to use a tart dressing of oil and lemon on the fish to cut the sweetness.

> 250g (2 medium) onions, cut in half and sliced
> 2 tbsp extra virgin olive oil
> 2 bay leaves
> 1 sprig of thyme
> 1 sprig of rosemary
> 1 tbsp honey
> 1 tsp white wine vinegar
> salt and plenty of pepper

In a covered pan, cook the onion in the oil with the bay leaves, thyme and rosemary over a very low heat for about 30 minutes, stirring occasionally, until the onion is very soft and just beginning to colour. It will stew in its juice rather than fry.

Add the honey, vinegar, salt and pepper and cook over medium heat for another 10 minutes or until much of the liquid has evaporated.

Stuffed Fish | serves 4

Ask the fishmonger to scale and clean a bream or sea bass weighing about 1.5kg and to remove the bones through the back. Or have the fish filleted with the head left on one of the fillets. Brush the fish with 2–3 tbsp extra virgin olive oil and season lightly inside and out with salt and pepper. Stuff with Onion Fondue with Honey (page 190) or Garlic Purée (see page 185) and place in a baking dish. Pour on the juice of ½ lemon or about 4 tbsp dry white wine. Put under the grill for 5–6 minutes until the skin is crisp and brown. Then bake in a pre-heated 190°C/375°F/Gas 5 oven for 20–25 minutes or until the flesh flakes easily away from the bone when you cut it with a pointed knife.

Roast Fish | serves 8

Any large fish is suitable for this recipe. Sea bass is the grandest fish of the Mediterranean, but a large bream is marvellous too.

> 1 sea bass or bream weighing about 2.5kg
> 6 tbsp light extra virgin olive oil
> salt and pepper
> juice of 1 lemon
> 6 tbsp dry white wine

Pre-heat the oven to 190°C/375°F/Gas 5.

Brush the fish with 1–2 tbsp of the oil and season lightly inside and out with salt and pepper.

Place in a baking dish with a mixture of the lemon juice, the remaining oil and the white wine.

Put under the grill for 5–6 minutes until the skin is crisp and brown, then bake for about 35 minutes or until the flesh begins to flake away from the bone when you cut it with a pointed knife.

Variation

For a Moroccan variation marinate the fish for 30 minutes in the following mixture, blended in a food processor: a bunch of coriander, a bunch of flat-leafed parsley, 3 crushed garlic cloves, salt, 6 tbsp extra virgin olive oil, ½–1 tsp ground ginger, and ¼–½ tsp saffron powder.

Marinated Fish | serves 10

Fish lightly cured in salt and marinated in olive oil, lemon juice and herbs is a tradition in the Mediterranean. In the old days a variety of fish were used. These days in France, salmon – not a Mediterranean fish – has been adopted as the popular one for this treatment. Start the night before you plan to serve. It is important to use very fresh fish.

> *2 salmon fillets, together weighing about 1kg, with the*
>   *skins left on*
> *3 tbsp coarse sea salt*
> *200ml light extra virgin olive oil*
> *juice of 1 lemon*
> *a large bunch of mixed herbs including chervil, chives*
>   *and dill, chopped*

Carefully remove any small bones from the fillets (tweezers will help). Sprinkle the fillets with the salt, on the skin side as well as inside.

Put the fillets together to re-form the fish and place in a large deep plate that can hold the liquid when it is drawn out. Cover with cling film and leave in the refrigerator for about 12 hours, turning the salmon over when the juices start to collect.

Scrape off the salt with a spatula and wipe the fish with paper towels, then rinse the fish in cold water under the tap. Taste a piece. If it is too salty, soak it in fresh water for as long as it takes to get rid of the saltiness. Mix together the oil, lemon juice and herbs and pour into the bottom of 1 or 2 large dishes. Lay the fillets, flesh side down, on this marinade and refrigerate, covered with cling film for about 3 hours.

Before serving, cut diagonal slices across the grain of the fish – they can be very thin or fairly thick.

Variations

The fish is also delicious marinated in the herbs and olive oil alone, with no lemon.

Serve with a sauce: Salsa Verde (see page 186); Aïoli (see page 274–5); or Tarator (page 187). It is also lovely served with the raw tomato sauce, Sauce Vierge (page 183).

Tip

Do not use fine salt as it penetrates the fish and makes it too salty, instead of drawing out the juices.

Pan-Cooked Fish Fillet

Cooking filleted fish in a large heavy pan or Spanish *plancha*, or on a thick metal sheet, barely filmed with oil, is currently the most popular way in France. It is also the easiest. The French call it *poêlé*. It is fashionable to cook the fillet on one side (the skin side) only. The result is a wonderfully moist, juicy texture. You can use any fish fillet, large or small, but it must have the skin on. Sea bass fillets and whole sides of salmon cook beautifully in this way. Scoring the thick part on the skin side prevents curling and allows the fish to cook evenly.

Oil the pan or sheet and heat it to just below smoking point. Brush the fish with oil and sprinkle with salt. Place it, skin side down, in the pan, and cook, uncovered, over a medium heat. It will gradually cook through to the top. The fish is done when it becomes opaque right through and the flesh flakes easily. When cooking a thin fillet, the heat can be quite fierce. A thick piece is best done over a gentle heat. A fat salmon fillet can take more than 20 minutes. Some people like to finish by putting the fish, brushed with oil, under the grill for a few seconds.

If you do not have a very large frying pan or *plancha*, cut the fillets into manageable pieces.

Serve sprinkled with parsley and accompanied with a sauce such as Salsa Verde (see page 186), Romesco (page 188–9), Aïoli (page 274–5), Tarator (page 187), Sauce Vierge (page 183) or Onion Fondue with Honey (page 190).

Grilled Fish

Cooking fish over charcoal is an old and enchanting way of doing things in the Mediterranean.

For fish steaks, use tuna (currently very fashionable), swordfish, hake, turbot, cod, haddock or halibut. Simply brush the fish with olive oil and sprinkle with salt and pepper. Place about 5cm from the fire, on a well-oiled grill over glowing embers, or under the oven grill. Cook for 2–4 minutes on each side. The fish is cooked when the flesh flakes away from the bone when you cut with the point of a knife. It is important not to over-cook. The best way to cook tuna is to sear it on the outside at high heat (close to the fire) and to leave it underdone inside.

For whole fish, use small or medium-sized bream, gurnard, red mullet, sardines and also flat fish such as sole and skate. Have them scaled and cleaned but keep the heads on. Brush with extra virgin olive oil and season with salt and pepper. Cook for 2–5 minutes on each side, depending on the size. Cut into one fish with a pointed knife to see if they are done.

For fish fillet (large fish split along the backbone), use sea bass, bream, hake, swordfish, turbot, salmon. Leave the skin on. Brush with extra virgin olive oil and season with salt and pepper. Cook on the skin side only, not too close to the fire, and do not turn the fish over or it will dry out. It does cook through.

Serve grilled fish with a dressing or sauce. Dress with Oil and

Lemon Dressing (see page 181), adding, if desired, chopped herbs such as fennel, thyme, marjoram, oregano, or tarragon, or try Warm Lemon and Tomato Dressing (see page 182). Accompany with any of the sauces featured between pages 183 and 190 and lemon wedges.

Deep-Fried Fish

Deep-frying is the most popular way of cooking fish in the Arab world. The method was introduced to Spain and Sicily by the Arabs in the early Middle Ages. Southern Italians excel at their *fritti misti* – a medley that may include red mullet, sardines, anchovies, whitebait, fillet of sole, baby hake, baby squid and large prawns. The Andalusians are the world's best at frying any kind of fish and seafood. Many people these days are averse to this method of cooking, but the result is delightful and worth trying.

To ensure success you must follow these rules:

- Use olive oil to fry because it can reach high temperatures without deteriorating (it can be filtered and re-used).

- There must be enough oil to cover the fish and the temperature should remain constant. Always start frying at high heat to seal the fish, then turn the heat down to moderate if necessary.

- Use a large, deep pan so that there is no risk of the oil bubbling over.

- Fry fish of about the same size together.

- Season the fish with salt inside and out and cover entirely, but lightly, with flour.

- Small fish must be fried very briefly at a very high heat so that they are crisp and brown but still moist inside.

- Larger fish take longer (3–4 minutes on each side) and need a lower temperature so they have time to cook inside before the skin gets burnt.

- Fish steaks or fillets are best first dipped in seasoned flour then in lightly beaten egg for extra protection.

- When frying, turn only once, lift out and drain on paper towels.

- Prawns, squid and fat mussels are usually dipped in batter before frying. To make a batter for 500g seafood to serve 4 people, mix 120g flour with 1tsp baking powder, ½ tsp salt, 2 tbsp olive oil and 150ml water. Beat well and let it rest for 30 minutes.

Poached Fish in White Wine | serves 4

Poached fish – fillets or steaks – are good to serve hot or cold.
You may use any white fish. The saffron is a Mediterranean
touch which you occasionally find in various countries.

> *150ml dry white wine*
> *150ml water*
> *2 bay leaves*
> *a few parsley stalks*
> *a little salt and white pepper*
> *a pinch of saffron (optional)*
> *4 fish steaks or fillets*

Put all the ingredients except the fish in a pan wide enough to
contain the fish in one layer. Bring to the boil and lower the
heat to a simmer.

Add the fish and simmer gently for 3–6 minutes, depending on the thickness and type of fish, until the flesh is opaque
and flakes when you cut into it with the point of a knife.

Serve with Oil and Lemon Dressing (see page 181).

Accompany with Salsa Verde (page 186), Sauce Vierge (page
183), Garlic Purée (page 185), Mayonnaise or Aïoli (see page
274–5), or Tarator (page 187).

Variation

This is a simple and marvellous Italian way with fish: fry 1 chopped garlic clove in 4 tbsp extra virgin olive oil over low heat. Add 150ml dry white wine and 2 chopped tomatoes. Bring to the boil and add the fish fillets. Simmer for 5 minutes. Add 1tbsp chopped flat-leafed parsley and serve in a soup bowl with some of the liquid

Sautéed Fish | serves 4

This is a quick and easy way to cook fish fillets. Another advantage is that you can incorporate herbs and spices.

> *4 fish fillets*
> *25g/2 tbsp butter*
> *1 tbsp sunflower or vegetable oil*
> *salt and pepper*
> *aromatics (see below)*

Sauté the fish in a mixture of sizzling butter and oil, adding salt and pepper and aromatics, for about 5 minutes or until the fish turns opaque and begins to flake. Turn the fillets over once.

Aromatics

For a Moroccan flavour, add ⅓ tsp powdered ginger and ¼ tsp saffron to the pan with the butter and oil.

For another North African flavour, add 1tsp ground cumin, 1 tsp paprika, ¼ tsp cayenne, the juice of ½ lemon and a good bunch chopped coriander.

For a touch of southern France, add 2–3 tbsp chopped fennel leaves and 1 tbsp Pastis.

For another Moroccan variation, add ½–1 Preserved Lemon Peel (see page 272), rinsed and cut into small pieces, 8–12 green olives (pitted if preferred) and 2 tbsp capers.

Fish Cooked in Pastry | serves 8–10

This is a Mediterranean version of a *poisson en croûte*. Salmon and sea bass are both suitable; ask the fishmonger to fillet and skin the fish for you.

> *2 × 500g packets of frozen puff pastry, defrosted*
> *1 large egg, separated*
> *2.5 kg salmon or sea bass*
> *3 tbsp sunflower or vegetable oil*
> *juice of ½ lemon*
> *salt and white pepper*

Pre-heat the oven to 230°C.450°F/Gas 8.

The pastry packets are divided into two pieces of dough, each weighing 250g. Stick two pieces from one packet together and roll out into a long, thin piece, about the thickness of a coin. Cut out in the shape of the filleted fish but slightly larger, adding a tail. Save any leftover pastry for decoration.

Lay the fish shape on a damp baking sheet and leave it in a cold place to rest for 15 minutes. Brush it with the egg white to prevent it from getting too soggy with the fish juices, and prick it all over with a fork so that it does not puff up unevenly.

Bake it for 8 minutes or until crisp and lightly coloured. Turn it over, brush the other side with the egg white, put it back in the oven and bake for a few more minutes until this side is golden. Let it cool.

Brush the fish fillets with the oil and lemon juice and season with salt and pepper. Place them on top of each other on the baked pastry.

Roll out the remaining pieces of dough, sticking them together to make one large sheet, the thickness of a coin, that will cover the fish.

Cover the fish entirely with the dough, and cut round it, leaving a margin of about 2.5cm, including around the tail.

Using a rounded knife, lift the edge of the baked pastry base and tuck the dough margin underneath, pressing gently to seal.

Decorate the pastry. Using a teaspoon, make a scale design on the body. Using the leftover scraps of dough, attach thin ribbons to represent the tail, gills and fins and stick on a little ball for the eye.

Brush all over with the egg yolk and bake for 15 minutes until puffed up and golden. Then lower the heat to 150°C/300°F/Gas 2 and bake for another 30 minutes.

If the pastry seems to brown too quickly, cover it with foil or with slightly dampened greaseproof paper.

Serve accompanied with Fresh Tomato Sauce (see page 271), adding the ginger, or with Warm Lemon and Tomato Dressing (see page 182).

Red Mullet in Tomato Sauce | serves 4

This dish looks beautiful, red on red.

> 4 garlic cloves, chopped
> 4 tbsp light extra virgin olive oil
> 500g (about 6) ripe tomatoes, peeled and chopped
> salt and pepper
> 1½ tsp granulated sugar
> 4 lemon slices
> 4 red mullet, weighing about 1kg in total, scaled and
>   cleaned but with the heads left on
> 12 black olives, pitted (optional)
> 3 tbsp chopped flat-leafed parsley

In a large frying pan that can hold the fish in one layer, fry
the garlic in the oil over low heat until it just begins to colour.
Add the tomatoes, salt, pepper, sugar and the lemon slices and
simmer for 10 minutes, then put in the fish and the olives, if
using, and simmer for 4 minutes or until the fish flakes easily
away from the bone. Add the parsley before serving.

Creamy Fish Flan with Spicy Tomato Sauce

serves 8 or more

This fish dish – a delicately flavoured creamy flan, served with a hot peppery sauce -- is from Provence. It is the kind of dish you can easily make for a lot of people. You may use one type of fish only or a variety of firm white fish such as cod and haddock, as well as salmon. Buy fish fillets and have them skinned.

1 litre milk
1½ tbsp tomato purée
¼ tsp saffron
8 large eggs
salt and white pepper
butter, for greasing
750g potatoes, peeled and sliced
1.5kg fish fillets, cut into 4cm pieces

For the sauce
4–5 garlic cloves
*½–1 red chilli pepper, finely chopped, or a good pinch of
    cayenne*
2 tbsp extra virgin olive oil
2 × 400g tins Italian chopped tomatoes
salt
1–2 tsp granulated sugar

Pre-heat the oven to 180°C/350°F/Gas 4.

In a saucepan over medium heat, bring the milk to the boil. Dilute the tomato purée with a little of the milk and add it to the pan along with the saffron.

Beat the eggs in a bowl then gradually beat in the hot milk. Add salt and pepper to taste.

Grease a 36cm baking dish with butter. Arrange a layer of potatoes at the bottom, then add a layer of fish, sprinkling lightly with salt. Pour the milk and egg mixture over the top.

Place the dish in an oven tray and pour water into the tray up to the level of the custard so that the flan cooks *au bain-marie*. Bake for 1–1¼ hours or until the custard sets.

Meanwhile make the sauce. Fry the garlic with the chilli pepper in the oil until the aroma rises. Add the tomatoes, salt and sugar and cook for 10 minutes.

Serve the flan hot, accompanied with the sauce.

Fish Couscous with Quince | serves 8

This delicious Moroccan-inspired couscous is best made with skinned fillets of a firm white fish such as cod, haddock or whiting.

For the couscous
500g couscous
600ml warm water
½–1 tsp salt
3–4 tbsp groundnut oil or light vegetable oil

For the fish
4–5 garlic cloves, chopped
3 tbsp groundnut or vegetable oil
1kg plum tomatoes, peeled and chopped
salt
2 tsp granulated sugar
1–2 chillies, cut open and deseeded
2.5cm piece of ginger peeled and cut into small pieces
750g (2 large) quinces
1kg fish fillet, skinned

Pre-heat the oven to 200°C/400°F/Gas 6.

Soak and prepare the couscous in a baking dish according to the directions on pages 111–12, cover with foil and set aside.

Fry the garlic in the oil until it just begins to colour. Add the tomatoes, salt, sugar and chillies. Crush the ginger pieces in a garlic press over the pan to extract the juice, discarding the pressed ginger. Simmer over low heat. Peel, core and slice the quinces and add them to the pan immediately, before they turn brown.

Cook, covered, for 15–30 minutes or until the quinces are tender. The time varies depending on the size, quality and ripeness of the fruit. Remove one or both of the chillies when you think the sauce is spicy enough.

About 20 minutes before serving, put the couscous, still covered with foil, in the oven to heat through.

About 5–10 minutes before serving, add the fish to the sauce and simmer until the flesh begins to flake. Bring the fish stew and couscous to the table in separate serving dishes. Serve in soup plates, the couscous first and the stew on top.

Tip

Quinces are a very hard fruit and you will need a large sharp knife to cut them.

Skate with Cumin and Potatoes | serves 4

All over North Africa, cumin is the standard flavouring for fish. Small skate, tender enough to fry quickly, should be used for this Tunisian dish. The wings are bought already dressed from the fishmonger.

> *4 garlic cloves, crushed*
> *1½ tsp ground cumin*
> *salt*
> *about 100ml extra virgin olive oil*
> *4 small wings of skate weighing 1kg in total*
> *500g (about 4–5) new potatoes, boiled and sliced*
> *pepper*
> *2 tbsp capers*
> *1 lemon, quartered*

Mix together the garlic, cumin, salt, and 3–4 tbsp of the oil. Cut the fish into pieces about 5cm wide, cutting in between the long soft bones, and rub the pieces with the garlic mixture.

In a large frying pan, fry the fish pieces in batches in shallow oil, giving them about 4 minutes on each side, until the flesh begins to flake away from the bone. Transfer to a baking dish, cover with foil and keep warm in the oven.

Sauté the potatoes slowly in the same oil, adding salt and pepper and the rest of the oil, and turning them over until they are lightly golden. Add the capers towards the end.

Serve the fish hot on a bed of the sautéed potatoes, with the lemon wedges.

Variation

Pieces of skate from a large fish can be used but they must first be boiled for about 10 minutes.

Sautéed Prawns with Cognac | serves 2

Cooked king prawns are common in supermarkets now, but if you can get hold of uncooked frozen ones, they are even better. This makes a luxurious dish for two. Large uncooked prawns need shelling and de-veining. To do this, remove the black thread that runs the length of the prawn with a sharp knife.

> *2 garlic cloves, chopped*
> *125g peeled cooked king prawns or about 10 uncooked*
> *   prawns*
> *2 tbsp extra virgin olive oil*
> *salt and pepper*
> *1½ tsp tomato purée*
> *3 tbsp cognac*

Sauté the garlic and the prawns for 30 seconds in the oil, stirring, until the pre-cooked prawns are heated through or until the uncooked ones turn pink. Add salt and pepper, the tomato purée and cognac and cook for a further 30 seconds. To serve, you can ignite the sauce and flambé it, if you wish.

Mussels with Garlic and White Wine | serves 4–6

Fashionable Belgian mussels-and-chips restaurants in Paris serve mussels in thirty different ways, but the classic and simple *moules à la marinière* is how people still choose to make them at home in the south of France.

> 2kg mussels
> 2 garlic cloves, finely chopped or crushed
> 2 tbsp extra virgin olive oil
> 500ml dry white wine
> black pepper
> a handful of flat-leafed parsley, chopped

Prepare the mussels (see pages 261–3).

In a very large pan, fry the garlic in the oil until it just begins to colour. Add the white wine and boil for 5 minutes.

Add the mussels and plenty of pepper. Cover the pan and cook over low heat for about 2 minutes – until the mussels open. Immediately remove from the heat.

Discard the mussels that did not open. Use a slotted spoon to transfer the mussels to serving bowls or soup plates. Strain the winey mussel broth through a thin muslin or fine strainer and pour a little into each bowl. Sprinkle with the parsley.

Baby Squid with Garlic and Chillies | serves 4

> 500g small squid
> 2 garlic cloves, chopped
> 1 red chilli, deseeded and very finely chopped
> 3 tbsp extra virgin olive oil
> salt and pepper
> 1 tbsp lemon juice
> 1 tbsp chopped flat-leafed parsley
> 1 lemon, cut in wedges

Clean the squid and cut the body pouches into rings (see page 261).

Sauté the garlic and chilli pepper lightly in the oil over low heat.

When the garlic begins to colour, add the squid. Season with salt and pepper and sauté briefly over medium heat, turning over the pieces, for 2–3 minutes only. Sprinkle with the lemon juice and parsley and serve at once, accompanied with the lemon wedges.

Pasta with Prawns | serves 4

Some years ago the *Sunday Telegraph* asked me to do a piece on the favourite dishes of famous Italians. I had to call Luciano Pavarotti, Claudio Abbado, Armani, Valentino and other personalities – chasing them around the world. Most of them said that their favourite food was the seafood pasta they made themselves. One or two used unorthodox ingredients such as champagne or a little curry and cream, but most were purists, preferring the classic dishes with prawns or mussels. This pasta can also be made with mixed seafood.

> 3 garlic cloves, finely chopped
> 3 tbsp extra virgin olive oil
> 1 hot red chilli, deseeded and finely chopped, or a very
>   good pinch of chilli powder (optional)
> 500g (6 medium) ripe tomatoes, peeled and chopped
> 250ml dry white wine
> salt and pepper
> 1–2 tsp granulated sugar or to taste
> 400g spaghettini, tagliolini, or tagliatelle
> 500g fleshy shelled cooked tiger prawns
> 4 tbsp finely chopped flat-leafed parsley

Fry the garlic in the oil until it just begins to colour. Add the chilli and tomatoes, and cook for 5 minutes.

Add the wine. Season with salt and pepper, add the sugar and simmer for 10 minutes to reduce.

Cook the pasta in plenty of boiling salted water until al dente.

Add the prawns to the sauce and heat through when the pasta is ready, and stir in the parsley.

Pour the sauce over the pasta and serve.

Variations

Make the sauce without tomatoes and add about 170ml double cream at the end.

For a mixed seafood pasta use 70g mussels and 250g small squid, cleaned and cut into rings (see page 261) with 200g prawns.

Spaghetti with Mussels in White Wine | serves 4

Clams are often used rather than mussels, but mussels make sense because they are more fleshy. Here they are *in bianco*, that is, without tomatoes, which best preserves the pure flavour of the sea. Linguine may be used instead of spaghetti. Do not serve grated cheese – Parmesan or other – with this dish.

> *1kg mussels*
> *170ml dry white wine*
> *400g spaghetti or linguine*
> *salt*
> *2–4 garlic cloves, chopped*
> *6–8 tbsp extra virgin olive oil*
> *black pepper*
> *5 tbsp chopped flat-leafed parsley*

Clean and prepare the mussels (see pages 261–3). Put them in a large pan, with about half the wine. Cover and cook over a high heat for about 1 minute. Take the pan off the heat as soon as the mussels open. Discard any that remain closed. Strain the juices from the pan and reserve.

Cook the spaghetti in plenty of vigorously boiling salted water until al dente.

Meanwhile, heat the garlic in 1tbsp of the oil over low heat until it begins to colour and the aroma rises. Add the strained mussel juice and the rest of the wine and oil and boil vigorously for a few minutes to reduce. Add pepper.

Drain the spaghetti as soon as it is al dente. Mix well with the sauce, sprinkle with pepper and plenty of parsley and serve with the mussels on top. Or you may mix the drained spaghetti in the pan with the mussels before serving.

Scallops with Balsamic Vinegar Dressing

serves 2

The secret of cooking scallops is to cook them as briefly as possible. They make a royal first course, served on a bed of Mixed Green Leaf and Herb Salad (see page 22), using the dressing in this recipe.

> *For the dressing*
> *6 tbsp light extra virgin olive oil*
> *2 tbsp balsamic vinegar*
> *salt and pepper*
>
> *½ quantity Mixed Green Leaf and Herb Salad (page 22)*
> *8 scallops*
> *1 tbsp light vegetable or extra virgin olive oil*

Combine the dressing ingredients and use half the mixture to dress the green salad.

Wash the scallops and pull away the intestinal thread. Cook them in a greased frying pan for 30–40 seconds on each side. Serve hot on a bed of the dressed salad with a drizzle of dressing on each.

Moroccan Fish Salad | serves 4

500g (about 5) new potatoes
salt and pepper
500g firm white fish fillet, such as cod, haddock or
    monkfish
2 tbsp white wine vinegar
6 tbsp light extra virgin olive oil
1mild onion, red or white, finely chopped
2 tbsp capers
a good bunch coriander, chopped

Boil the potatoes in salted water until tender, then drain, peel
and cut into 2.5cm pieces.

Poach the fish in boiling salted water for 5 minutes or until
it just begins to flake when you cut it with a knife. Let it cool
and flake it into similar-sized pieces.

Beat the vinegar and oil with a little salt and pepper and pour
over the fish and potatoes in a serving bowl. Add the rest of the
ingredients and mix gently. Allow to cool before serving.

Seafood and Rice Salad | serves 4

Made in large quantities, this is an ideal dish for a party. It is relatively cheap, beautiful to look at, can be prepared in advance, and tastes delicious. The seafood may include a firm-fleshed white fish, cut into pieces and poached; squid cut into rings and poached; peeled cooked prawns; and mussels, in or out of their shells. (For poaching fish see page 196; for preparing mussels and squid see pages 261–3.)

> 250g American long-grain rice
> salt
> 4–6 tbsp light extra virgin olive oil
> juice of 1 lemon or to taste
> pepper
> 4 spring onions, finely chopped
> a large bunch flat-leafed parsley or a mixture of herbs such
>   as chives, mint and coriander, chopped
> about 500g poached fish or seafood, such as white fish,
>   squid, prawns and mussels

Cook the rice in boiling salted water for about 18 minutes until just tender, then drain.

Dress while still warm with the oil, lemon juice, salt and pepper. Let it cool and mix with the spring onions and parsley or mixed herbs. Fold in the seafood.

Serve cold. You may like to accompany with Mayonnaise or Aïoli (see page 274–5) but it is not essential.

Variations

A ring of cold Tomato Risotto (see page 107) filled with a variety of poached seafood dressed with Oil and Lemon Dressing (see page 181) or with (cold) Lemon and Tomato Dressing (see page 182) is a spectacular variation.

Roast Pepper, Tomato, Tuna and Bread Salad

serves 4

Tunisia's famous salad *meshweya* (it means 'grilled') becomes a hearty summer's day meal when it is served on a bed of bread soaked with tomato juice and vinaigrette. Use a white rustic or country loaf. Adding Harissa is traditional, but I prefer this simple dish without.

For the soaked bread base
4 slices country bread, about 1.25cm thick
175ml tomato juice
5 tbsp extra virgin olive oil
2 tbsp red or white wine vinegar
salt and pepper
½–1 tsp Harissa (optional) (see page 268)

For the salad topping
2 green or red peppers
3 ripe medium tomatoes
1 × 200g tin of tuna, drained and flaked
3 hard-boiled eggs, quartered
4–8 black olives
1–2 tbsp capers, squeezed of their vinegar
    (optional)
1 × 50g tin of anchovies, drained (optional)
3–4 tbsp extra virgin olive oil

juice of ½ lemon
salt and pepper

Cut the crusts off the bread and toast it. Arrange the slices side by side in a 23cm wide shallow bowl.

Mix the tomato juice, olive oil, vinegar, salt and pepper, and Harissa, if using, and pour over the bread so that it is thoroughly soaked.

To make the salad topping, place the peppers and tomatoes on a baking tray under the grill, turning them occasionally, or cook them on the barbecue.

Take the tomatoes out as soon as their skins come off easily. Peel and cut them into quarters. Take the peppers out when their skin is blackened in parts and blistered. Skin them, following the directions given on page 263, and cut them into ribbons about 1.25cm wide.

Arrange the elements of the salad – the peppers, tomatoes, tuna, eggs, olives, capers and anchovies, if using, – on the soaked bread in a decorative way.

Mix the oil, lemon juice, salt and pepper and drizzle over the top.

Italian Fish Soup | serves 6–8

This is a dish for a party. I have made it with whole fish –
bream, gurnard, red snapper, whiting and red mullet – which
looks dramatic but is difficult to serve and there is the problem
of bones to deal with. It is far easier to use fish fillets, such
as monkfish, cod, turbot and red mullet. You can make it
with fish fillets alone or you may add prawns and scallops or
mussels.

1 bottle (750ml) dry white wine
1.5 litres water or fish stock (you may use stock cubes)
2 fresh red chillies, deseeded
5 garlic cloves, slivered
1kg new potatoes
1kg plum tomatoes, peeled and cut in half, or 2 × 400g
*   tins peeled plum tomatoes*
4 bay leaves
a few parsley stalks
salt to taste
5 tbsp extra virgin olive oil
1.5–2kg fish fillets
500g shelled king prawns (optional)
6 scallops (optional)
1kg mussels, cleaned and steamed open (see pages 261–3)
*   (optional)*

Put the wine and water or fish stock in a large pan. Add the chillies, garlic, potatoes, tomatoes, bay leaves, parsley stalks, and salt and bring to the boil. Simmer for 20 minutes.

Add the oil and the fish fillets and cook for 5–10 minutes until they just begin to flake when you cut into them with a pointed knife. Add the prawns, scallops and the mussels in their shells, if using, and cook for a further 30 seconds.

Serve in soup bowls with toasted bread rubbed with garlic. You may put the bread at the bottom of each soup bowl to soak up the broth.

Tunisian Fish Soup with Potatoes | serves 4

There are fish soups with potatoes and tomatoes in all the countries around the Mediterranean. What is different in each area is the type of fish used and the aromatics. This simple version is a meal in itself. Its appeal is the herby and peppery aromatics. Start with only a little Harissa (see page 273) or chilli pepper and add more later, if you wish. I prefer it not too peppery. Hake is often used in Tunisia for this soup, but you can use any firm white fish such as cod, haddock, or turbot.

500g potatoes, cut into thick slices
2 medium tomatoes, peeled and quartered
1 litre water
½ tsp paprika
¼ tsp Harissa (see page 273) (or more to taste) or a good
    pinch of chilli pepper
½ tsp cumin
3 garlic cloves, chopped
juice of ½ lemon
salt
3 tbsp extra virgin olive oil
500g white fish fillets, skinned
a large bunch flat-leafed parsley or coriander, finely
    chopped
3–4 sprigs of mint, finely chopped

Put all the ingredients except the oil, fish and herbs together in a pan. Simmer for 25 minutes or until the potatoes are tender.

Stir in the oil and add the fish. Cook another 10 minutes. Then gently break up the fillets into smaller pieces and add the herbs.

Serve hot with toasted bread.

Fish Soup with Saffron and Cream | serves 4

This delicate creamy soup with the flavours of the south of France is one of our family favourites. It is extremely easy to make with boneless fish fillet such as cod, haddock, whiting or other white (non-oily) fish, or, if you like, with a mixture of fish and cooked prawns. Serve it with warmed or lightly toasted bread.

25g butter
1 tbsp sunflower or light vegetable oil
1 medium onion, chopped
3 garlic cloves, finely chopped
1 medium leek, sliced
1 celery stick, sliced
250ml dry white wine
500ml water
salt and white pepper
a 7cm strip of orange peel
200g (1 medium-large) potato, cubed
½ tsp saffron threads
600g skinned fish fillet
150ml double cream

Heat the butter and oil in a large saucepan. Add the onion, garlic, leek and celery and sauté lightly until they are soft and beginning to colour slightly.

Pour in the white wine and water. Season with a little salt and pepper and add the orange peel. Simmer for 10 minutes.

Add the potato and cook for 20 minutes, adding water if necessary as the liquid evaporates. Add the saffron and fish fillets and cook for 8–10 minutes or until the fish turns opaque. Cut the fish into pieces.

Remove the orange peel, stir in the cream and cook for 1–2 minutes. Serve hot.

Variation

Replace about 200g of the fish with cooked prawns. Add them to the pan just before you add the cream.

Desserts

The usual Mediterranean way to end a meal is with fruit: figs, grapes, apricots, dates, melons and watermelons, peaches, plums, cherries, apples, pears or oranges. Simply bring a bowl to the table, or peel and cut up a selection and arrange it on a platter. Another tradition is to offer dried fruit and nuts with coffee. Most of the desserts in this chapter are made with fruit to celebrate the Mediterranean's rich bounty. I have provided quite a few recipes – because I love desserts, and because they are all-important at dinner parties.

Macerated Fruit Salad | serves 4

Leaving the fruit to macerate in a mixture of lemon and sugar releases their juices and gives them a richer, more intense flavour. Use a good variety of fruit, such as bananas, oranges, apples, pears, apricots, strawberries, raspberries, blueberries, seedless grapes, kiwis, cherries, mangoes and pineapple.

> *a variety of fruit (about 1kg), peeled if necessary*
> *4 tbsp granulated sugar, or to taste*
> *juice of ½–1 lemon*

Cut the fruit into pieces or leave them whole if small. Layer in a large bowl, sprinkling each layer with sugar and lemon juice. Allow to macerate for at least an hour.

Variation

Instead of lemon juice, sprinkle with 4 tbsp cognac or kirsch.

Orange Slices in Syrup | serves 8–12

This preserve makes a ready sweet to serve with a dollop of thick double cream.

> *1kg oranges, cut into 0.5cm slices*
> *500g granulated sugar*

Put layers of orange slices and sugar in a pan. Cover with water and cook gently for 1½ hours, adding water to keep the fruit covered.

When cool enough to handle, press the orange slices into a jar and cover with the syrup. Store in the refrigerator (where they will keep well for weeks).

Variation

If you want the orange slices to keep for several months, use twice the amount of sugar.

Fresh fruits poached in sugar syrup make an easy sweet. For a more glamorous dessert they can be served on a bed of Rice Pudding (see pages 243–4) or on an Almond Custard (pages 246–8).

> *1kg fruit – choose 2 or more from the following: apples, pears, peaches, plums, greengages, apricots, gooseberries, cherries and grapes*
> *450ml water*
> *100–250g granulated sugar*

Wash the fruit; peel, halve and stone it if necessary. Apples and pears should be peeled, cored and sliced.

To make the syrup, bring the water to the boil with the sugar. Start by using the lesser amount of sugar and add more during the cooking after tasting. The sweetness of the syrup is a matter of taste and the tartness of the particular fruit.

Put the fruit in the boiling syrup. Each fruit needs a different cooking time, which also depends on their degree of ripeness. Ripe fresh fruit should be poached very briefly. Cherries, gooseberries and grapes need only 1–3 minutes, apricots and plums require 5 minutes; peaches 10; apple slices 10–15 minutes; clementines with their peels (cut in half) may need 25 minutes; and pears, if they are unripe and hard, need more than 40 minutes. Orange slices and tangerines can be cooked for 1 hour. For mixed compotes it is best to poach the fruits separately or to add them at different times so that none is overcooked. Serve cold or chilled.

Variations

As special flavouring, add to the syrup the peel of a lemon or an orange, the juice of ½ lemon, a stick of cinnamon, a few cloves or a vanilla pod or a few drops of vanilla essence (extract).

At the end, add a few tablespoons of kirsch, cognac or Cointreau.

Instead of water, you could use a mixture of wine – red or white – and water.

Stewed Quince | serves 4

You will find this all over the Mediterranean, but in Turkey it is the most popular dessert. It is one of my favourites.

> *700g (2 large) quinces*
> *250g granulated sugar*
> *750ml water*
> *150ml clotted or thick double cream*

Cut the quinces in half through the core. They are very hard and you need a sharp knife and strong pressure to cut them. Trim the blackened ends, but leave the cores and seeds – they will provide a lovely characteristic jelly.

In a wide shallow pan, put the sugar and water (there should be enough to cover the quinces in one layer) and bring to the boil. Put in the fruit, cut side down, and simmer, covered, until it feels tender when you pierce it with the point of a knife. The cooking time can vary between 20 minutes and 1 hour depending on the quality and ripeness of the fruit.

Lift out the fruit and place it on a dish. When it is cool enough to handle, cut out the cores carefully. Boil down the syrup, uncovered, to a thick consistency (thick enough to coat the back of a spoon) – it turns a rich garnet red.

Return the fruit to the pan, cut side down, and cook in the syrup for 10 minutes.

Arrange in a serving dish, cut side up, with the syrup poured over. Serve with a dollop of cream in the centre, or pass the cream round so that people can help themselves.

Peaches in a Fragrant Syrup | serves 4

These peaches are not too sweet; they have a very delicate vanilla and ginger flavour. There must be enough syrup to cover them and it can be re-used – to make another quantity if necessary. Use large yellow peaches that are firm and not too ripe

> *1 litre water*
> *250g granulated sugar*
> *¼ tsp ground ginger*
> *few drops vanilla essence*
> *4 large yellow peaches*

For the syrup, boil the water and sugar until the sugar is dissolved. Add the ginger and vanilla essence and remove from the heat.

To skin the peaches, drop them in boiling water (off the heat) and leave for a few minutes. Drain the peaches and slip off the skins. Poach the peeled peaches, whole, in the syrup for 15–20 minutes, until very tender. Leave them in the syrup until you are ready to eat. Serve chilled or at room temperature, without the syrup.

Serve with Almond Custard (see pages 246–8) flavoured with a sweet wine such as Beaume de Vin de Pêches, with cassis or with Honey Ice Cream (see page 249).

Roast Peaches | serves 4

This very simple and delicious way of preparing peaches is from southern Italy.

> *8 peaches, cut in half, unpeeled, and stones removed*
> *120ml Amaretto or Marsala*
> *2–3 drops vanilla essence*
> *4 tbsp granulated sugar, or to taste*

Pre-heat the oven to 190°C/375°F/Gas 5.

Arrange the peaches in a shallow baking dish, cut side up. Mix the Amaretto or Marsala with the vanilla and 2 tbsp of the sugar, and pour over the peaches, so that a little settles in the hollows.

Bake for 10–20 minutes or until soft (the time varies, depending on the size and ripeness of the fruit).

Sprinkle the tops with the remaining sugar and put under the grill until caramelized. The baking can be done in advance, but the last step must be carried out just before serving.

Poached Fruit on a Rice Pudding Base | serves 6

Mastic and rose water – two Arab flavourings – give the rice pudding a delicious exotic flavour that marries well with the poached fruit topping. Mastic is a resin from a tree which you can buy in small 'grains' or crystals in Greek and Middle Eastern stores. You have to pound it yourself to a powder, with a little sugar, with a pestle and mortar. You must use very little as otherwise the taste is unpleasant. An alternative to mastic is ground cardamom, which is easy to come by and easier to use.

For the rice pudding
200g round Italian or pudding rice
350ml water
1 litre milk
175g granulated sugar, or to taste
2 tbsp rose water
½ tsp ground mastic

For the fruits poached in syrup
250g granulated sugar
250ml water
juice of ¼ lemon
3 peaches or nectarines, peeled and quartered
3 pears, peeled and quartered
6 apricots, pitted and cut in half

To make the rice pudding, put the rice in a large pan with the water. Bring to the boil and simmer for 8 minutes or until the water is absorbed. Add the milk and simmer over very low heat, stirring occasionally, for about 30–45 minutes until the rice is very soft and the milk is almost, but not entirely, absorbed. Add the sugar and stir until dissolved, then add the rose water and the mastic and stir vigorously. Pour into a wide shallow serving dish.

To make the fruit poached in syrup, put the sugar, water and lemon juice in a pan and bring to the boil, then simmer gently. Pour boiling water over the peaches or nectarines to loosen their skins, then peel them.

Put the different fruits in the syrup separately, in batches, because they cook at different rates. The time also depends on their size and degree of ripeness. Peaches and apricots can take 6 minutes only, and pears much longer. Turn the fruit pieces over once if they are not entirely covered by the syrup.

As they become tender, lift them out of the syrup on to a plate, to drain the excess syrup. Arrange them in a flower pattern on top of the rice pudding. Serve cold.

Variations

For an alternative flavouring, add 1 tsp ground cardamom at the same time as the milk and omit the mastic.

For alternative Fruit Compotes, see pages 237–8.

Cherry Clafoutis | serves 4

This old Provençal country dish of cherries baked in custard remains popular. There is no need to pit the cherries, but you can do so if you prefer.

> *500g black cherries*
> *3 large eggs*
> *100g caster sugar*
> *1 tbsp plain flour*
> *2 drops vanilla essence*
> *2 tbsp Calvados or kirsch*
> *150ml double cream*
> *100ml milk*
> *icing sugar to sprinkle on*

Pre-heat the oven to 180°C/350°F/Gas 4.

Wash and dry the cherries. Put them in a buttered shallow 22cm baking dish.

Beat the eggs with the sugar and flour. Add the vanilla and Calvados or kirsch, and gradually beat in the cream and milk.

Pour the mixture over the cherries and bake for about 45 minutes or until the cream sets and a light golden crust forms.

Serve warm, sprinkled with the icing sugar. You may put it under the grill for 1 minute until caramelized.

Sautéed Fruit with Almond Custard | serves 6

One of my favourite summer desserts is an assortment of fruit poached in syrup (see page 233) on an almond custard served chilled. In the winter, sautéed fruit on steaming hot custard is an irresistible sweet. All kinds of fruit can be sautéed. Grinding blanched almonds yourself in a food processor will give a better texture than using bought ground almonds. The almond essence is optional; in the past, the almond flavour was intensified by adding a few bitter almonds.

For the sautéed fruit
75g/6 tbsp unsalted butter
3 apples, peeled and cut into small pieces
2 pears, peeled and cut into small pieces
6 apricots, pitted and cut into pieces
a dozen or more cherries
3–4 tbsp granulated sugar, or to taste
3 tbsp Calvados or Armagnac

For the almond custard
175g granulated sugar
5 large egg yolks
75g plain flour
500ml milk
2–3 tbsp kirsch, rum, Calvados or Armagnac
100g ground almonds
3 drops almond or vanilla essence (optional)

To prepare the fruit, melt the butter in a large frying pan and sauté the apples and pears, stirring and turning them over occasionally, for 15 minutes, or until they are tender. Add the apricots and cherries and sauté briefly, until soft. Add the sugar and alcohol and cook for a few more minutes.

To make the custard, beat the sugar with the egg yolks to a light pale cream. Then beat in the flour.

Bring the milk to the boil in a heavy-bottomed pan. Very gradually pour on to the egg mixture, beating vigorously until well blended, then pour the mixture back into the pan.

Simmer for 3 minutes longer, stirring constantly so that lumps do not form and the cream does not catch at the bottom. If the cream does slightly burn at the bottom, be careful not to scrape the burnt bits into the custard.

Stir in the alcohol, almonds and the almond or vanilla essence if using. Be careful to add only a few drops of almond essence, as too much is horrible. Cook for a few more moments.

Pour into a wide shallow serving dish and spoon the fruit with their juices all over the top.

If you want to prepare the custard in advance, pour the custard into a baking dish and heat it through in the oven. Pour the hot fruit on top just before serving.

Variations

Serve the almond custard cold topped with poached fruit (see pages 233 and 242–3).

Serve the cold almond custard as a bed for raw fruit, such as strawberries, raspberries, blueberries, white and black grapes, pitted fresh dates, sliced kiwi fruit and orange slices cut into small pieces.

Honey Ice Cream | serves 6

This fragrant ice cream is a speciality of Provence where it is made with lavender honey.

500ml milk
4 large egg yolks
150g lavender, acacia or other clear, perfumed honey
150ml double cream
1 tbsp orange blossom water

Boil the milk. Beat the egg yolks to a pale cream, then beat in the honey, the cream and, finally, the hot milk.

Return the mixture to the pan and stir with a wooden spoon over low heat until it thickens to a light cream, but do not let it boil or it will curdle. Then stir in the orange blossom water.

Let it cool and pour into a serving bowl. Cover with cling film and freeze overnight or at least 5 hours before serving. You may serve the ice cream straight from the freezer.

Pear Granita | serves 4–6

> *250ml water*
> *150g–200g granulated sugar*
> *juice of 1 lemon*
> *1kg (5) pears, peeled and cored*
> *Poire William liqueur or a fruit brandy (optional)*

In a wide pan that can hold the pears in one layer, boil the water and sugar with the lemon juice until the sugar melts. (Put in the lesser amount of sugar to start with and add more, if necessary, at the end, depending on the sweetness of the pears).

Put in the pears, and cook, covered, for 10 minutes or until they are soft.

Blend the pears with the syrup to a cream in a food processor. (Taste for sugar and add more if necessary.) Pour into ice cube trays, cover with cling film, and leave the pulp to freeze hard overnight in the freezer.

Put the frozen cubes, in batches, in the food processor and process them into a very fine, frothy slush. Pour into a serving bowl and serve at once or return to the freezer, covered with cling film.

Take out 10 minutes before you are ready to serve. If you like, pass around the pear liqueur or fruit brandy for people to help themselves to a drizzle.

Apricot Granita | serves 4–6

This water ice has a refreshingly tart flavour.

> *250ml water*
> *200g granulated sugar*
> *juice of ½ lemon*
> *1kg ripe apricots, pitted*
> *kirsch or fruit brandy (optional)*

Boil the water and sugar with the lemon juice in a wide pan until the sugar melts.

Put in the apricots and cook, covered, for 5 minutes or until they are very tender.

Blend the apricots with their syrup to a cream in a food processor. Pour into ice cube trays and cover with cling film. Let the pulp freeze hard overnight in the freezer.

Put the frozen cubes, in batches, in the food processor and turn them into a very fine, frothy slush. Pour into a serving bowl and serve at once or return to the freezer, covered with cling film.

Take out 10 minutes before you are ready to serve. If you like, pass around the kirsch or fruit brandy for people to help themselves to a tablespoon or so.

Frozen Apple Fool with Calvados |

This is called a *parfait* in France.

>   *2 large Golden Delicious apples, cored and sliced*
>   *150ml fruity dry white wine*
>   *100g caster sugar*
>   *3 large egg yolks*
>   *3 tbsp Calvados*
>   *150ml double cream*

Put the apples and the white wine in a pan and simmer with the lid on for 5–10 minutes until the apples are soft. Remove the lid and cook on a higher heat to reduce the liquid.

Add half the sugar, mash the apples with a potato masher or fork, and cook, stirring, until the apple purée is thick and most of the liquid has disappeared.

Beat the egg yolks with the remaining sugar to a pale cream. Pour over the apple purée, off the heat, stirring vigorously, then stir over low heat for 30 seconds. Stir in the Calvados and chill in the refrigerator.

Whip the double cream to firm peaks and fold into the cold apple purée. Pour into a bowl lined with cling film – this makes turning out easier. Cover the top with cling film and leave to freeze overnight.

Serve the fool straight from the freezer. Remove the cover-

ing cling film, turn out on a serving plate, and remove the
remaining cling film.

Variations

Add 3 drops vanilla essence, a small stick of cinnamon and
2 cloves.

Pears may be used instead of apples, with kirsch or Poire
William.

Semi-Freddo with Marrons Glacés | serves 4–6

This is a splendid and luxurious sweet. Italian food stores sell broken pieces of marrons glacés, which work out very much cheaper than the usual product.

> *4 large egg yolks*
> *150g caster sugar*
> *300ml single cream*
> *4 tbsp Armagnac or cognac*
> *300ml whipping or double cream*
> *200g marrons glacés, cut into small pieces*

Beat the yolks with the sugar to a pale light cream. Bring the single cream to the boil, remove from the heat and beat it into the egg mixture.

Return the mixture to the pan and cook, stirring constantly over low heat, without letting it boil or it will curdle, until the cream is thick enough to coat the back of a spoon.

Add the Armagnac or cognac to the custard, let it cool, and put in the freezer for 1 hour, covered with cling film.

Beat the whipping or double cream until stiff and fold it into the cold custard, then fold in the marrons glacés.

To shape the ice cream into a dome that is easy to unmould, line a bowl with cling film and pour the mixture in, cover with another piece of cling film and freeze overnight.

Remove the cling film and turn out just before serving.

Frozen Cream with Prunes and Armagnac

serves 4

This light chantilly-type cream with a strong flavour of Armagnac is easy to make and tastes delicious.

>   200g Californian pitted prunes
>   85ml Armagnac brandy
>   300ml whipping cream
>   2 tbsp caster sugar
>   2 drops vanilla essence

Chop the prunes coarsely in a food processor, add the Armagnac and soak for an hour.

Beat the whipping cream until it forms peaks, then beat in the sugar and vanilla essence and fold in the prunes and Armagnac.

Cover with cling film and freeze for at least 4 hours. You can serve the cream straight out of the freezer.

Sweet Couscous with Nuts and Dates | serves 4

Couscous is the Berber food of North Africa. This sweet couscous is more of a breakfast dish or afternoon snack than an after-dinner dessert. It is tasty and satisfying comfort food.

> *250g medium couscous*
> *about 300ml water*
> *6 tbsp granulated sugar, or to taste*
> *2 tbsp groundnut or sunflower oil*
> *125g mixed nuts, such as walnuts, blanched almonds,*
>   *hazelnuts, pistachios and pine nuts*
> *½ × 225g box California dates, pitted and cut into pieces*
> *300ml hot milk*

Pre-heat the oven to 200°C/400°F/Gas 6.

Put the couscous in a round ovenproof serving dish. Boil the water with 4 tbsp of the sugar and all of the oil. Pour over the couscous and stir well. Leave for about 15 minutes, stirring occasionally, until the water has been absorbed.

Rub the grain between your hands to remove any lumps that stick together. Add more sugar if it is not sweet enough to your taste.

Toast the nuts very lightly under the grill or in a dry pan and chop them coarsely. Stir them into the grain with the dates. Cover the dish with a lid or with foil and heat through for 20 minutes in the oven. This will have a steaming effect.

Heat the milk and serve the couscous hot, accompanied by the milk and extra sugar for people to pour over it.

Note

You may heat the couscous in a saucepan with a lid instead of in the oven, but you will need to stir it often so that it does not burn at the bottom.

Apricot and Almond Pudding | serves 6

Apricots give this old Provençal speciality a refreshing tartness.

> 100g softened unsalted butter
> 3 large eggs
> 150g caster sugar
> 150g coarsely ground blanched almonds
> 2–3 drops almond essence
> 1kg apricots, pitted and cut in half
> 2 tbsp icing sugar
> pot of double cream, to serve
>
> **For the sauce**
> 200g apricot jam
> 3 tbsp water
> 1–2 tbsp kirsch or apricot brandy

Pre-heat the oven to 180°C/350°F/Gas 4.

Blend the butter and eggs with the sugar in a food processor. Add the almonds and almond essence and continue to blend to a soft cream. Pour into a 30cm baking dish.

Arrange the apricot halves on top, cut side down, pressing them into the paste. Bake for about 45 minutes or until the paste is firm and lightly coloured.

To make the sauce, heat the apricot jam with the water and

kirsch or apricot brandy and stir until it melts. Let the sauce cool.

Serve the pudding cold, sprinkled with icing sugar. Accompany with the sauce and a bowl of cream.

Variation

Use pears, peeled, cored, cut in half and boiled for about 15 minutes or until almost tender, instead of apricots.

Ricotta Cake | serves 8

This rich Sicilian cake is a bit like a soufflé. The orange blossom water is a legacy of the old Arab occupation of the island.

> 500g ricotta
> 150g caster sugar, or to taste
> 5 large eggs, separated
> 2 tsp orange blossom water
> grated zest of ½ lemon
> 75g diced candied orange peel

Pre-heat the oven to 180°C/350°F/Gas 4.

In a food processor, blend the ricotta, sugar, egg yolks, orange blossom water and grated lemon zest to a homogenous cream.

Fold in the diced candied orange peel.

Beat the egg whites until stiff, then fold into the ricotta mixture.

Pour into a greased and floured, preferably non-stick 20cm cake tin and bake for 45 minutes or until brown on top. The cake rises quite high. Let it cool before turning out.

Variation

Use a few drops of vanilla essence or 1½ tsp cinnamon instead of orange blossom water.

Chocolate Cake | serves 6

This has such a wonderful creamy soft texture that it is more of a pudding than a cake.

> *100g dark bitter chocolate*
> *50g unsalted butter*
> *4 large eggs, separated*
> *100g caster sugar*

Pre-heat the oven to 150°C/300°F/Gas 2.

Melt the chocolate and butter in a heatproof bowl over a pan of boiling water.

Beat the egg yolks and the sugar to a pale light cream, then beat in the chocolate mixture.

Beat the egg whites until stiff and fold them into the chocolate and egg mixture.

Pour into a buttered, preferably non-stick 20cm cake tin and bake for 30 minutes. Leave it in the oven for 30 minutes before turning out (it comes out easily). Let it cool before serving.

Moroccan Almond 'Snake' | serves 12 or more

This is a good pastry to make for a party. It is very rich, so serve it in small pieces. It takes its Moroccan name *m'hencha* from the world *hencha*, meaning 'snake', because it looks like a curled snake.

> 500g ground almonds
> 200g caster sugar
> 1½ tsp cinnamon
> 3 drops (no more) almond essence (optional)
> 2 tbsp orange blossom water
> 4 large egg yolks
> 5 sheets of filo pastry
> 3–4 tbsp unsalted butter, melted, or sunflower oil
> icing sugar, for dusting

Pre-heat the oven to 180°C/350°F/Gas 4.

In a bowl, mix the ground almonds, sugar, ½ tsp of the cinnamon and the almond essence, if using. Add the orange blossom water and 3 egg yolks, and combine well with your hands.

Open the packet of filo only when you are ready to use the pastry. Take out 5 sheets and keep them in a pile. Brush the top one lightly with melted butter.

Press the almond paste with your hand into long thin sausages the thickness of a thumb, and place them end to end, making a rod of paste along one long edge of the filo sheet, about 2cm from the end.

Lift the pastry edge up over the paste and roll up into a loose, long thin roll. To curve this roll without tearing the pastry, wrinkle the pastry first by pressing the ends of the roll gently towards the middle.

Lift the pastry roll carefully on to the middle of a greased flat ovenproof dish or a sheet of foil on a baking tray, and curve it gently into a snail shape.

Continue in the same way with the rest of the filling and sheets of filo, placing the long, wrinkled rolls end to end, curving them to make a long coil.

Brush the top with the remaining egg yolk mixed with a teaspoon of water, and bake for 45 minutes until crisp and browned on top.

Serve cold, dusted with the icing sugar and a sprinkling of the remaining cinnamon.

Basics

Preparations

To Clean and Prepare Squid

Pull the head away from the body pouch and discard the soft innards that come out with it. Discard the insides of the pouch – the inkbag, if any, the icicle-shaped transparent cuttlebone and the soft innards. Keep the tentacles in their bunches but remove the eyes and the small round cartilage at the base of the tentacles by cutting with a sharp knife just above the eyes (be careful that ink doesn't squirt out at you from the eyes). Rinse thoroughly. Cut the body into rings.

To Clean and Prepare Mussels

Scrub the mussels, pull off the beards and wash in several changes of cold water. Test to see if they are alive: discard any that are broken and those that are too heavy or too light, or do not close when they are tapped or dipped in cold water. To steam them open, put them in a large pan with a finger of water and the lid on. Take off the heat as soon as they open (in about 1 minute). Discard any that remain closed.

To Roast and Peel Peppers

Many dishes call for roasted peppers. Choose fleshy peppers. Put them on an oven tray under the grill, about 9cm from the grill (or grill them on the barbecue). Turn them until their skins are black and blistered all over.

Alternatively, it is easier to roast them in a 180°C/350°F/ Gas 4 oven for 1 hour (or the hottest oven for 30 minutes) until they are soft and their skins begin to blister and blacken. They need to be turned once during the roasting. To loosen the skins further, put them in a pan with a tight-fitting lid or in a strong polythene bag and twist it closed. Leave for 10–15 minutes. This helps to loosen the skins. When the peppers are cool enough to handle, peel them and remove the stems and seeds. Reserve the juice that comes out and strain to remove the seeds as the juice can be used as part of the dressing.

Roast peppers can be kept, covered with oil, for several months. Store them in a cool, dark place.

To Grill or Roast Aubergine Slices

These days many people prefer grilled or roasted aubergines to fried ones, but very often they are not cooked enough.

Cut the aubergines into 0.5–1cm slices, lengthways, or into rounds, sprinkle with salt and let them degorge their juices for half an hour. Rinse and dry them. (This process can be omitted if the aubergines are not particularly bitter – it is not always necessary.) Brush both sides generously with oil and turn under the grill or over a charcoal fire.

Alternatively, lay them on an oven tray and bake in a very hot oven until tender and lightly browned.

To Prepare Hearts of Small Globe Artichokes

With a small sharp knife, cut off the stalk and cut away or pull off the tough outer leaves, starting at the base, until you are left with the pale inner leaves. Then slice off the tough ends of these, open them out and scoop out the prickly inner choke with a pointed spoon.

To Prepare Bottoms of Large Globe Artichokes

Cut away all the leaves to the bare flat bottom with a sharp pointed knife, then cut or scrape away the chokes from the centre.

Vinaigrette

In the Mediterranean lemon juice is often used in a salad dressing instead of vinegar.

> *salt and pepper*
> *1 tbsp white or red wine vinegar or lemon juice*
> *3½ tbsp light extra virgin olive oil*

Stir the salt and pepper into the vinegar until the salt is dissolved. Then beat in the oil.

Fresh Tomato Sauce | makes enough to serve 4–6

This sauce can be used for many dishes including sautéed fish and pasta.

> *1–2 garlic cloves, finely chopped or crushed*
> *2–3 tbsp extra virgin olive oil*
> *8 ripe plum tomatoes, peeled and chopped*
> *salt and pepper*
> *1–2 tsp granulated sugar*

Sauté the garlic lightly in the oil over low heat until the aroma rises. Add the tomatoes, salt, pepper and sugar and simmer for 10–15 minutes to reduce slightly.

Variations

Add 3 tbsp chopped parsley or basil.

Add 1 tbsp fresh grated ginger or the juice of a 2.5cm piece of ginger, peeled and crushed in a garlic press.

A Moroccan version uses ½ tsp ground ginger, ¼ tsp saffron and ¼ tsp chilli pepper. It is sometimes garnished with 6 or 7 olives and ½ chopped Preserved Lemon Peel (see page 272).

Preserved Lemon Peel

This preserve, often used chopped up as a garnish, gives an unusual mellow lemony flavour to many North African dishes, from salads to seafood.

Wash the lemons and make two vertical cuts in a cross, almost but not quite through the lemons, so that the sections still hold together at the stem. Sprinkle about 125g salt for 1kg (about 8) lemons inside on the cut flesh, then close them and pack them tightly in a clean jar. Squeeze enough fresh lemon juice over them to cover. The salt will draw out the juices and the peel will soften within a week. Cover and store in a cool dark place. They will be ready to use in 3–4 weeks.

Rinse off the salt before using and discard the flesh. It is the peel alone that you want.

Variation

Another way of making preserved lemon peel is to cover the lemons with water and add a protective layer of oil on top.

Harissa | makes about 225ml

This hot chilli paste is used in many North African dishes.

50g dried hot red chilli peppers (stems and seeds removed)
4 garlic cloves, peeled
1 tsp ground caraway
1 tsp ground coriander
about ½ tsp salt
extra virgin olive oil

Soak the chilli peppers in water for 30 minutes until soft. Drain and pound with the garlic, spices and a little salt with a pestle and mortar, or blend in a food processor, adding just enough oil, by the tablespoon, to make a soft paste. Press the mixture into a jar and cover with oil. This way it keeps very well, for several weeks, in the refrigerator.

Mayonnaise and Aïoli | makes about 400ml

Aïoli is the garlic mayonnaise common to Spain and southern France. It is made in the same way as mayonnaise but with added garlic. It is used as a dip for crudités, and with boiled vegetables or fish and seafood. It is best not to use olive oil alone as the result is too strong and overpowering. Instead, use a mixture of a bland vegetable oil and olive oil. The proportions may vary. I like to use ⅔ vegetable oil and ⅓ olive oil. It is usual to beat the garlic with the egg yolk first until pale and creamy but you may prefer to add it at the end when you can taste and decide how much you want to put in.

To ensure success, all the ingredients must be at room temperature (do not use an egg straight from the refrigerator) and the bowl should be warm.

> *1 large egg yolk*
> *juice of ½–1 lemon*
> *½ tsp salt*
> *300ml oil – a mixture of sunflower or light vegetable oil*
> *with extra virgin olive oil*
> *4 garlic cloves or more, to taste, crushed in a press or*
> *pounded to a paste (if you are making aïoli)*

Put the egg yolk in a warmed bowl (place it on a wet cloth to prevent it from slipping). Add some of the lemon juice and the salt.

Add the oil, a little at a time – first drop by drop, then in a thin stream – beating vigorously all the time with an electric whisk.

As the oil becomes absorbed the sauce will thicken to a heavy, thick consistency.

Finally, beat in the garlic and the rest of the lemon juice, to taste.

Variation

For a *rouille*, which goes very well with fish soup, add 1–2 tsp paprika and a good pinch of cayenne pepper.

Focaccia | serves 6–8

Flatbreads are very common throughout the Mediterranean region. They are usually quite soft, often flavoured with herbs or spices and sometimes embellished with ingredients such as chopped olives, fried onions and tomato pulp. In the Arab world they can be sprinkled with sesame, fennel, caraway, anis or onion seed, or with mixtures of thyme, sesame and ground sumac. My favourite for making at home is the versatile Italian focaccia, made with olive oil, which has become immensely popular in Britain and the United States. This recipe is for basic focaccia. Several variations follow.

> *1 tbsp active dry yeast*
> *pinch of granulated sugar*
> *about (a little less than) 450ml lukewarm water*
> *750g strong white flour*
> *2 tsp salt*
> *5 tbsp extra virgin olive oil (plus a little to grease the*
> *dough and pan)*

Dissolve the yeast and sugar in about half the measured warm water. Leave for 10 minutes until it froths.

Put the flour and salt in a large bowl, and make a well in the centre. Pour in the yeast mixture and 3tbsp of the oil and mix with a wooden spoon.

Add the remaining warm water very gradually – just enough

to make a soft ball that holds together, mixing first with the wooden spoon, then working it in with your hand.

Turn on to a lightly floured surface and knead for about 10 minutes until very smooth and elastic, adding a little flour if too sticky, or a drop of water if too dry.

Pour a little oil in the bowl and turn the dough in it to grease it all over. Cover the bowl with cling film and leave to rise in a warm place for about 1½ hours or until doubled in bulk.

Index

lemon
  green vegetable soup with
      68–9
  oil and lemon dressing 181
  preserved lemon peel 272
  warm lemon and tomato
      dressing 182
lentil(s)
  brown lentils and rice with
      caramelized onions
      51–2
  chick pea and lentil soup
      69–70
  red lentil soup 66–7
  and spinach salad 31–2
lettuce and orange salad 24
linguine with spinach and pine
    nuts 97–8

macerated fruit salad 235
marinated fish 194–5
marrons glacés, semi-freddo with
    254
mayonnaise 274
Mediterranean cuisine 3–17
melon soup, chilled 57
milk, pumpkin soup with 61–2
mint, salad of chopped cucumber
    and 25
Moroccan almond 'snake'
    262–3
Moroccan carrot salad with
    yoghurt 28

Moroccan fish salad 222
mushroom(s)
  with garlic and white wine
      44
  pasta and 93
  pie filling 76
  soup 63
  tart 86–7
mussels
  cleaning and preparing 267
  frying 200
  recipes
    with garlic and white wine
        215
    in white wine with
        spaghetti 219–20

nuts
  sweet couscous with nuts and
      dates 256–7
  see also almonds; chestnuts;
      pine nuts; walnuts

okra in tomato sauce 175
olive oil 13–16
  and lemon dressing 181
  potatoes mashed with parsley
      and 168
  vegetables cooked in white
      wine and 123–4
olives 12–13
omelettes
  aubergine 141–2

Index | **285**